WITHDRAWN

A SPECIAL
AND CURIOUS
BLESSING

A SPECIAL
AND CURIOUS
BLESSING

by

Cynthia Propper Seton

W. W. NORTON & COMPANY, INC.

NEW YORK

To the memory of my father

Karl Propper

Table of Contents

A SPECIAL
AND CURIOUS
BLESSING

The Canopy

When I view all beings not as special creations, but as the lineal descendants of some few beings which lived long before the first bed of the Cambrian system was deposited, they seem to me to become ennobled.

CHARLES DARWIN

If God took the earth, which was a waste and a void, and made order out of chaos, it was indeed a prime example. Men and women, we little gods and fishes, have to struggle to bring order out of chaos every day. This book is a reflection of my personal effort to impose an order on what I know of the world so that I can live in it. At the core it is about being a woman, and takes a positive view.

It seems egotistic to take oneself as a point of reference or at least immodest. Several years ago a magazine ran a sort of test of egotism that I did terribly well in. The fellow who devised it had monitored the speeches of famous people to see how quickly and how frequently they used the word "I." Richard Nixon was among the winners, and Mrs. Roosevelt was way down at the bottom. But she is my heroine. I thought when she died that in a world in which there is no Mrs. Roosevelt I do not wish to go on. It may therefore be understandable that I quail before my incessant use of "I," that I frequently try to reconstruct whole paragraphs to put the onus of thought upon a second or third person.

But I am the woman, the wife, the mother, the American who thinks these thoughts, and it usually seems somewhat more honest anyhow to take responsibility for them rather than foist them off as generalities or abstract truths. In an existential age there is a tendency to deny the reality of any person but the first. I am not altogether at home in this age, this half of the twentieth century. I like people and need people and don't find others more unreal than I sometimes find myself.

Without feeling actually optimistic about the future of mankind it does seem to me that today's Word—the message that there is no meaning, no purpose, no hope in life—has been oversubscribed. The rush to say nay conveys an eagerness to be too heartfelt about the bad things, and a sense of shame and unworthiness about acknowledging the good things. I may tend to reverse this emphasis.

I believe that to some extent you have to take life by the throat and make it work, but that you can't take people by the throat and make them attend. It said in *The New York Times* that the San Francisco hippies had only one rule which is, while you could think whatever you like, you couldn't ask anybody to listen. This is the way they tucked themselves into a cozy corner, but they lived too readily with chaos for me, and from my position as a sort of archhousewife the lives they led appeared to me not so much shocking and disorderly as boring.

I share with the hippies a distaste for being made to listen, but so does everybody else. Still, I am always listening with my eyes. I have a blind ear that gropes through music and poetry, but I hear very well what I read, and many times things that other people have written have marked my mind, caused me to veer, given me a heartening shove over the line. There may be a kind of person, probably in particular a woman, who is hovering at the line, who might find in this book the nudge to push her across and hence to move on. This is a satisfying idea to any writer and helps to mute if not to cancel the shame of presumption. For me, I must nervously admit that my nature contains something evangelical and even patriotic, and that in spite of coming from stock in which religion has been ruthlessly suppressed by modernism for a couple of generations, there is an exegetic quality to what I write. And I want somebody to listen.

I don't seem to be haunted by the big question, What is the meaning of it all?—and am spared, no doubt, a dismal answer. My absorption is with humankind, *little* gods, and little questions like, "For crying out loud, what are they doing now?" As to fishes, I mention fishes because of Darwin, and because it happens to many people who are readers that a book now and then will be especially pivotal, seminal. *The Origin of Species* is a recent example of this experience for me, although I know less about science even than I do about music and poetry. But as I read that book I seemed to excise the science, and caught simply the beginnings of an understanding of the fantastic intricacy and beauty and order and logic of the universe and all in it. This has suited me splendidly. I want order to be implicit and necessary, and also I do not like to see any man, who must by Darwinian definition be a creature of fantastic intricacy, reduced to a statistic, confined in a category. Or any woman. When I look at myself I find I am infinitely complex—not infinitely interesting, mind you, but an entity with layers and layers of selves, edges sharp and blurred, humors alternating and blending, and with an absolutely incalculable number of tiny causes making me what I am and/or think I am at any moment. And of all that massive accumulation of data that adds me up, a very small proportion is comprehensible, or entertaining, or worth recording. If that is I, that is everybody—many even less entertainingly composed.

In Western civilization, since the Renaissance at least, alienation and despair tend to be the lot of nearly all. In America today we are way ahead in this respect as in others, and with our hands on those marvelously mindless technological tools, we can take an individual, whose short-lived, impoverished, dull-witted ancestors were ground down in life, unrecorded in death, for millions of generations, and we can extinguish him. We can extinguish him physically and worse, we can extinguish his sense of self. In every generation opinion is divided over whether the remarkable progress that man has made since the time he was a little wiggle in the salty sea is a matter for mutual congratulations, or whether the monumental forces that plague him are not, in Frost's words, "the Lord's great big joke." In our generation there is added for our conjecture, beyond the fear that the whole race may be annihilated, the fear that our own individuality may be annihilated first. Given the enormous odds against us, there are no rational grounds for cheer; but I am temperamentally optimistic, and when I am not actually cut down by what I read in my morning's *Times,* I take to life with considerable relish. I feel this is, in part, because I have the good luck to be a woman. I believe that to be a woman in this country today is not, as some think, a liability but a special and curious blessing, though not an unmixed blessing.

There is in a woman's life a latitude and a rhythm and the gift of time that not only permit, but invite her to range through the most disparate experiences, while the pressures on a man cause him to sharpen, confine, narrow. She doesn't bear his lifelong handicap, labor under the world's singular insistence that *he* win the bread and *he* bring it home. There are seasons and cycles in a woman's life. She can be generous. If she is very advanced she may have long since picked off the last shred of sexual inequality, as I have, and left herself free to suffer every imaginable human inadequacy, as I do. Although I don't feel lesser than a man by virture of being female, I do feel different. It is from this bias that I see women, the ups and downs of girlhood, mine and our children's, the longish, low stretch of early marriage, and the steady rise to forty, which is as far as I've actually got, an interesting plateau from which you can see the past and not want to live it over, and see the future and not want to live it either, not so soon.

I write from the hearth, from the spine of family, and say nothing much one way or another about women's rights and working mothers per se. Antecedent to women's rights are the rights of the child (should a woman bear a child), because it has always been known, and is being documented ever more meticulously, that to neglect a growing child is irrevocably to destroy a man. It is a personal agony that the converse is not necessarily true.

This is not a how-to book. Yet I am in awe of what I owe to the innocent device of force-feeding one's mind, so much so that I feel compelled to tell a young mother who finds herself faltering, fears the gaps are growing in her life, to *read* through them. When in Doubt Read On is what would be cross-stitched on my sampler. To read, not really selectively but toward the farthest edges of what you believe to be your capacity, begins as a game, an inchoate, even a little desperate, ploy. I acknowledge the

15

seeming dilettantish quality to this socking away, but I must testify to the quiet seeding that takes place within you. It is germane to the clearing up of a misunderstanding about educated housewives and what they can do, and when they can do what. They cannot major in organic chemistry or political science, graduate *cum laude,* duck into marriage and motherhood for fifteen or twenty years, and come out at 40, the witching age, automatically ready to take a commanding position in their field. It *was* their field, and they *were* chemistry or government majors. In fifteen or twenty years you become somebody else entirely, either a residue with all the promise atrophied from disuse, or a woman whose mind and sensibilities have grown so considerably in the interim that an almost chemical change has taken place. It is an absolutely new phenomenon, this great class of women (of wit and wisdom) who at thirty-five or forty have already performed the generative role and are ready to live another complete cycle of life. It is a cycle, thanks to science and technology, that women have to live, ready or not.

It can be argued that modern woman from birth to death is in herself a new phenomenon in a world of new phenomena. In fact I believe that is what I am arguing. You might almost say that she is technology's greatest triumph. Liberated from the exhausting biological and historical impositions by the pill, the washing machine, and allied mechanical aids, she is her own mistress, her own master. But when I think of myself, the most unshackled of creatures, with the enormous freedom I have to go anywhere, be anybody, do anything, then I feel I must explain why I'm still washing windows and children and clothes, why I'm not called President, or Doctor, or even Your Highness—(A little boy from Nora's second grade drifted into our back yard the other day and Nora said, "Mama, I would like you to meet Steven. Steven, I would like you to meet Cynthia. We call her Mama.")—why I'm called Mama.

The thing is, I was slow about catching on to life's possibilities, nowhere slower than in the matter of population explosion, which I finally understood as a personal experience. A couple of years ago I was on the platform with a Planned Parenthood official who wondered, conversationally, how many children I had.

"Five."

"Well, I think it's odd they should have asked you," she said, with a shudder for my irresponsibility.

It does seem irresponsible. If we had understood the problem then as well as we do now we probably would not have had Jenny and Nora. We were lucky.

If, initially, fate flung me into the role of housewife, I have stayed of my own accord. I may one day combine it with an outside job. Hardly a challenge for someone so quick and clever with the washing machine, who stands so coolly at the controls of her third brand new unsatisfactory stove, twisting knobs on the instrument panel like a pilot bringing down a jet. In fact the stove may drive me out. But so far I've experienced my unprecedented freedom in a confined situation, in concordance with the concordance of contraries.

Of all the contraries, the one that is healthiest to know fastest in the event that you have children is that you are not only free to loose, in the matter of cultural tradition, but free to bind, and in fact you have to bind. For a child must grow in a positive context of dreams and hopes. He must feel love and pride and loyalty, and the mother, being much older, much more mature, and with a chiseled mind—I'll have to assume a chiseled mind—skillfully rejecting, condemning, as the world passes in review before her, has to provide for his understanding and appreciation and enjoyment all kinds of positive, admirable, hopeful explanations and descriptions of that very world. It's a real exercise sometimes. That child lives by the promise of growth and progress, inside himself and out, and he has to believe that his country, his family, his ball team, the profession he aims for, are filled with heroes acting gloriously, and that he can be a hero too if he obeys the rules. And meanwhile, she, his free and modern mother, who has outgrown childish illusions and is beyond many kinds of social and religious intimidation, must find and pass on at least symbolic truths from our cultural heritage lest she throw the baby out with the bathwater.

For the crux of being modern is that all the social rules by which one elects to live as citizen of a state or as member of a family are losing the authority of divine commandment. So that when any relationship deteriorates, becomes inimical, one no longer bows the head in passive obedience to the inscrutability of God and His mysterious ways; there is no longer any Higher Purpose to useless suffering. Our principles may have the command of the categorical imperative but they are not hinged to heaven. One can unhinge the imperative.

One can become unhinged in the process. A woman can free herself so thoroughly that she cannot return for renewal to what Erik Erikson calls that "reservoir of collective integrity from which the individual must derive his stature as a social being." I cannot, as unbeliever, go to church, but then I must be wise enough, articulate enough, to substitute something in its absence that will feed my children's minds with whatever stuff internalizes purpose, integrity, responsibility. If I turn my back altogether on the culture I live in, I also cut myself off, and inevitably my children too, from the heroes and causes that embody its ideals (St. Francis, Thomas Jefferson), from the intricate pattern of human relationships that it sponsors (marriage, family), and finally and fatally, from the multiplicity of experiences in love and loyalty that are bread and wine to the soul.

If you don't have children it is another matter. You can reject religion, its strictures, symbols, holidays, live indifferent to what your neighbors think, fight the Establishment, grab the tangle of demands upon your credulity and amuse yourself by unraveling it. You can nonconform from the time you get up in the morning and take apple brandy for your fruit drink until you kick the box before you go to bed. But if you are a mother, particularly if you are a free and modern mother, you have, to some extent, to play house.

How do you play house? Well it's a very subtle game, and takes at least two. "And the Lord said, It is not good that the man should be alone; I will make him an help meet for him." Helpmeet or helpmate is, according to Webster, a corruption of this. To be meet for each other, man and wife, on and on through time, it is a help if there is a touch of *folie à deux*. That's what the help is. Accordingly, in our marriage, we have made through the years, unwittingly usually, but also with frequent moments of fake fervor, a household with unique style, identifiably American and under debt to our personalized version of the Judeo-Christian morality. That "style" at its worst does not bear thinking on; our patriotism is sometimes nearly buried beneath criticism, and God alone knows how well we do with morality.

But children are not impartial critics of their home, and until they are quite grown up it doesn't dawn upon them that its style is a human concoction, infinitely improvable. A child thinks his family is the way Life is. Maggie came home from school one afternoon last year with an English assignment (7th grade) requiring an essay describing some object or some ceremony that is particularly dear to the whole family. "Everybody has something religious to write about except me. I mean, they have going to Mass on Christmas eve, or Jewish candles. At first I thought I'd do our pictures or our books, but I decided I'm going to write about the pig." The pig: it is a quite large glazed white pottery pig that we all bought together in Normandy for about seven dollars and that we lugged home through land and sea and air. It was made in a sort of roadside pottery barn and is meant to decorate your garden, and is entirely comparable in intent to our native pink plastic flamingos. I mention this at the risk of sounding arch: it's not a golden calf, only a pretty pig. On its underneath it had for a long time some of the dirt from the French yard it was standing in (due to the long distance between the living room and the kitchen sink), and in this regard it makes me think of Darwin. One way that species spread is by the dirt that clings to the claws of birds who fly long distances, sometimes over water. There can be seeds in that dirt. Of course, the pig being on a marble table top, I didn't expect much growth.

You have to have a hospitable environment for growth with people in particular. That somebody leads a satisfactory life is a marvelously meshed achievement, due about one hundred per cent to luck. Next to luck comes a certain minimum felicity in the relationship between the mother and father of whoever it is. In the case of modern and free parents it is harder—the lion having to lie down with the lamb, both being uncertain which is which. It has been customary to attribute the failure of many marriages to the fact that the husband grows up and grows out of a taste for his permanently childlike bride; she, who is still pink and rosy and cluck-clucking about in dirndl skirts and aprons in a timeless way, took to playing house too wholeheartedly. Perhaps one new phenomenon today is that a man may be overtaken by his wife instead. But probably that is not new. In any event, while it is more difficult to make a modern marriage work, it may be more interesting, and if there are children the stakes are very high.

We are still trying to slip sex education into the American public school curriculum, but really we must go much farther much faster. It is elementary that a child learn how babies are born, fundamental that he learn how babies grow, what they must have to survive to adulthood sound in mind. Nobody ought to leave school without understanding that you love a child spontaneously but that love in marriage is a matter of mutual growth. Time is the new dimension, the fourth dimension in the twentieth century. It's the fourth dimension in marriage and love too.

The hippies said that everybody in America either knows he's miserable or doesn't know, and they didn't want any part of it, not the free enterprise system, not Mother's Day, nothing. They were out. The reason why they didn't support the Civil Rights movement was that it comes to helping Negroes *in*. This is rather true. It is true that our warm support for the Civil Rights movement and the poverty program amounts to urging people out of a despondency due primarily to physical impoverishment into a despondency due to emotional impoverishment. If people were true to the categories we put them in I must say that I would feel these efforts to help to be totally insane. Instead of only partly.

It is not only the hippies, the fringe, that chafe under this blindly unacknowledged discrepancy between how unsatisfactory life in America is today, and how eagerly and warmly we want more and more people to join in it, share it. What is called the generation gap is caused by this discrepancy too. You may call a college senior brash, immature, rebellious because he means to spend next year in jail rather than in the infantry. But perhaps his is a mature decision, he has not opted out, as they say, has not slid easily into a tolerance of this discrepancy, this double standard of word and deed, whereas his parents may have.

In particular perhaps his mother is not mature for 40, to get back to women. If as much can be said for his father, they have failed—where it can be said they have failed—in tandem. But I would think, generally speaking, that the young who choose jail, Mississippi, the Peace Corps, that is to say, those who reach out, are probably in good shape, and that those who turn limp from fear rather than from courage, take pot and love in, or withdraw, are in bad shape. The number in trouble seems large, though one wonders who does the counting. But in respect to the emotional crippling of children it seems to me that women have been overblamed for the kinds of mothers they make, and underblamed for the failure of their marriages.

Writing about women or being one, you cannot help but be impressed by their overwhelmingly human quality, how they keep slipping out of their purely female context. Still, I never think of a woman who is doing some grand, efficient job in the professions, or in government, or in business, as being *merely* equal. On average I think of her as bringing womanly qualities to bear upon whatever it is she is doing and with whomever. Where this is not so, where women in authority lack the gentler touch, the lower pitch, I assume that everybody around is sorry.

However, I don't know much about lady executives. The successful women I know best have not found their sex a particular strain but a special source of insight. Their sense of humility—whenever it crops up—stems not from coming second but from the growth of their understanding of the tensions of man through the rearing of children. That is why they turn so naturally to the job of

moderating, soothing, why they are in the peac‹
ment in such numbers. Is it strange that women w
guide, admonish, instruct children, are capable of
ing those qualities in national and internation‹
that are so impulsive, so primitive, so uncharitable, ‹‹
recognizably those of an infuriated child who has lost his
self-control? Does she send that child back out into the
street to smash his enemy, annihilate him, beat him to a
pulp? Or does she discourage him from action that is
unworthy of him? When she is for peace it is not out of
the softness of her heart, but out of the sharpness of her
mind.

In fact I believe that in a country as sophisticated as
ours, with a system of universal education extending back
for several generations, that it isn't, or oughtn't to be, the
young students who are the wisest critics of our society,
but instead, a species of woman that's evolving some
more. There is great variability in this species. The
women in it, however they are differentiated in the
ledger by falling under Housewife, Executive, etc., are
equalized by the sometimes conscious need to take extraordinary initiative, by historical standards, to contrive a
semblance of structure and meaning in life. They regularly sweep the chaos back, keep their doubts in order,
but possibly because they are themselves arrangers of
environment, puffers of pillows, soothers, they are able to
take themselves out of a cool category and put themselves
and those who are their concern under their own warm
care. This is the sort of modern woman who manages best
as a new phenomenon and who is very likely to develop a
sense of *noblesse oblige*, a rippling outward of her sense
of responsibility. It is a woman whose prototype might be
discerned in Mrs. Roosevelt.

I can make this experience I have had as educated
housewife and mother sound as if it contains a formula for

success in that line of work. The only failures I record are those I am able to laugh at. However, I believe neither in one great big absolute nor in any formulas for small successes, little absolutes, though I have certainly yearned from time to time to be all of a piece, to be a consistent, ever-improving whole myself, and to merge with that larger benevolent universal good by which I try to live and in which I only sentimentally believe. Every intellectual advance I've made toward the affirmation of some small absolute has been stayed absolutely by my sense of the infinite complexity of all men and each issue. This is the product of Mind X Motherhood, the cross-fertilizing of domestic life with intellectual growth, the being at once autodidact and woman of the house. It is the rearing of children, the very act that makes some women humble before God, that makes me humble before something else, the ungraspable immensity of the fact of our existence.

I can't be a pacifist, although I am in despair over the war by which we are riven as I write. I would like to stand firm and pure for No Censorship, but I buckle. Total political freedom, complete sexual equality are static slogans and appear to me to interfere like static with the function of the mind. The fact is, when I think it over, that I have long since ceased to fall for a Definitive Answer, and I am always, every day, looking for lines to draw. The site of a line eludes the modern brain. What is pornography? When must you disobey the law? Does there remain any reason to pass on to one's daughters the age-old value of virginity? Do you have to be faithful in marriage? To all of which I have no answers—windy explorations, but no answers. A line never turns out to be a blood-red gash, clearly discernible, but an always shifting and largely invisible hypothesis, like an air current or a sea current, that somehow must be tentatively allowed to divide what is permissible from what isn't. The intellectual problem is how close you can come to describing a line like this by diagnosis, by legal definition, and perhaps it cannot be satisfactorily done in any serious instance. But the problem is *there*, in the searching for the site. The problem is not solved by absolutes like No Censorship or No Double Standard.

Meanwhile alongside this recurrence of *line*, which is, geometrically speaking, one dimensional, I find that I am regularly defending, sometimes feverishly, the concept of structure, which is three dimensional: structure in the personality, in the family, in the community. So that I have been struck very forcibly by the poetic rather than geometric idea of *time* as the fourth and crucial dimension in coping with today's crises, personal and universal. An adolescent needs the second decade of life for his growth to maturity. It is fateful to crop this *time* too short. Great quantities of extra *time* have abruptly been grafted on a woman's day and on a woman's life. A black man's self-respect, his place of equal dignity in the American mind, cannot wait upon the *time* customary to bring younger generations abreast of new social truths.

I have pounced dizzily upon this device of the dimensions of line, structure, and time to build this book, borrowing somebody else's convention, knowing no more about old math than new math, and now I am going to place these dimensions under a sort of Darwinian canopy that should leave any real scientist who strays into these pages dumbfounded by my presumption.

We know we are tampering dangerously with the balance in the human environment as regards the threats of nuclear fallout, of unchecked human reproduction, of pollution. But when you get right down to what a human environment is, you reach the family. What has taken me up from this vantage point is the centricity of woman as the superintendent or mistress of environment, and in particular do I wonder whether modern woman will be willing or able to see herself, her self-restraint, as indispensable to human survival.

CHAPTER 2

On Marriage
and Monogamy

The psychology of adultery has been falsified by conventional morals, which assume, in monogamous countries, that attraction to one person cannot coexist with a serious affection for another. Everybody knows that this is untrue.

BERTRAND RUSSELL

For the purpose of evolving the human race I think it must be said that the family, as an institution, has been more than handy. Wherever you find people, anthropologists assure us, there is sure to be some family structure behind them. This will no doubt continue to be true in the future. But would the reverse hold? And is it possible that family structure in the West may abruptly give way to all the centrifugal forces that always tear at it because the traditional, powerful buttressing that has always shored it up is itself disintegrating? By buttressing I mean of course religious and secular law and community pressure. And

27

by abruptly I mean to point to the case of the passenger pigeon. Suppose we are prey to the same sort of mechanism that extinguished the passenger pigeon. This bird, Jenny tells me, was in a condition of such critical over-population in America that, had not man shaken him by the millions from his nesting perches, natural forces would surely have devised some other check upon his growth. But man shook him, thereby repeatedly decimating the flocks. And, as each pigeon needed to be part of a huge flock and could not bear being part of a small flock, the species lost its spirit and died, all in a flash as geological time goes.

As to humans, the continued existence of a strong family structure does not depend upon rational argument for it. The rational argument wins hands down. But will the family remain upright on that account, or will it buckle anyway and we all lose spirit and die? I came across a short reference in the *Times* to a University of California psychiatrist who said that from his experience a happy marriage was the rare thing, that education did not seem to improve its chances, and that it was usually up to the woman to make it work or break it up. Oh, I thought, how like a man, how unfair, how unequal, how true.

How like a man to see these things from a man's point of view. One male friend of ours was telling me a little rhyme the other day, though he could not remember its source, but it was meant to crystalize in a couplet all the world's wisdom:

> Hogamus higamus
> man is polygamous,
> Higamus hogamus
> woman's monogamous. . . .

he crooned happily. He was a bachelor. (Nora asked her father at dinner what a bachelor was and her father, his eyes scanning us all swiftly, replied, "A bachelor is a rich man.")

Take monogamy. Central to the strong family is a bias in favor of monogamy—or say at least twenty years' worth of monogamy, sufficient to bring the young through the critical years of childhood. In our culture the absolute position of monogamy has depended on a reverence for the purity of woman and has been regarded as not only God's will, but is believed to coincide with her natural instinct. She is monogamous by nature, that is to say. This keystone has been sufficient to support all the beliefs about the sanctity of home, the husband's duty, the wife's subordination with all the legal and ecclesiastical apparatus we have lately been so irreverently dismantling. On top of everything is there turning out to be no keystone? Does woman seem to have no definite instinct for monogamy after all?

Using the word instinct in the popular sense you have to figure women for at least two, the one being the mothering and the other being sexual. Until today the pressures to satisfy both inside the family have been enormous. Now we are all conditioned to believe that women have always been suppressed and repressed and presently depressed as a consequence of masculine arrogance and its petty vindictiveness. But I wonder after all if it wasn't the female in our species that charted the strict marital rules originally and devised the innumerable restrictions, obligations, codicils that appear variously throughout history, and thereby created that "hospitable environment" which allowed the race to survive and flourish. We know that to protect her young our female can be fierce as any tigress. To keep her children safe she has allowed man to lapse, but not marriage. I wonder, that is, if woman hasn't mothered the myth of her own monogamous instinct intuitively and whether, on becoming all-over modern and free and equal she will rashly explode it?

Can she devise a hearth for her young, perhaps according to some split level design, that will permit them to grow up safe and sane while also allowing her to remain unbound and uncommitted? It is hard to see how this could be done. I am not modern enough, haven't an easy enough taste for free association, to imagine a way. In fact I am just the sort of relic that is inclined to foster the myth of woman's monogamous instinct while not believing it.

I saw this clearly in my own reactions to a kind of classical conundrum that began one evening when a second friend of ours (male) asked if we knew why Hera had struck Tiresias blind. No we didn't, and what follows is not mentioned in the few source books that surround my desk, although the *Oxford Companion to English Literature* says "Tiresias, a Theban soothsayer, was struck by blindness for reasons variously given." This variation is that Tiresias as a young man had come across two snakes in the act of copulation and was thereupon transformed into a woman. He passed seven years as a woman and then saw two more snakes copulating and his manhood was immediately restored. Because of his having uniquely experienced the two human conditions, Zeus and Hera called him to settle an argument. The argument was over who enjoyed sexual pleasure more, man or woman, and Tiresias said it was woman. Thereupon Hera, in a rage, struck him blind, and Zeus, in order to mitigate the harshness of her act, since he was unable to undo it—a rule of Olympus—gave Tiresias the gift of foresight.

This piece of mythology fascinated the men among our friends in particular because Hera's rage seemed inexplicable to them. Why would she not have been pleased? Why wouldn't she have crowed over Zeus, Zeus whose episodes of infidelity to her were predicated on the belief that the male sexual need, in contrast to the female, was really extra-marvelous and irrepressible. I found myself half sharing their surprise at Hera and half in sympathy with her, and I stayed silent. Then an old man who was a philosopher said philosophically, "Perhaps Hera was the first Puritan"; and so the conversation drifted to other things.

Whatever philosophic or psychoanalytic meaning this myth has is beyond my competence to ponder, but if it really is an old story, then the ancient symbols may be woman's symbols, just meant for woman's mind. Zoologically speaking, a creature who is monogamous mates with but one of the opposite sex, and it is becoming increasingly hard to believe that the human female, by this definition, has this instinct unwatered. If this were true you would have to say that she was implicitly, temperamentally, and irreversibly monogamous, like the greylag goose Konrad Lorenz writes about, a notion that is today scarcely to be credited. Perhaps it is a notion that has never been credited by women, a notion only meant to comfort and contain men.

It is my belief that, generally speaking, woman is sexually aroused every bit as grippingly as man if not entirely similarly. She is also endowed with the contrary and perhaps more sustained need to care and to nurture her children, primarily her children. But this need to care spills over and is one of the things that accounts for her capacity to love and be loyal to one man. It supplements her desire for him, and then they are kneaded together by the response her attention invites. It is something that really happens between two people, but it is encouraged and expected to happen, surrounded and reinforced as it is by all the panoply of cultural tradition. But it doesn't have to happen, this love and loyalty and mutual and permanent taste for each other. The upper side of life has historically maintained the expectation, while the nether side of life has historically provided an escape, at least for the men. This is what is changing now. The nether side is surfacing. Or to put it differently, all the cards are being laid out on the table, and can we still play this game?

This digging inside for truth, this need to tell all, to be frank and open, to be painfully, brutally honest, this determination not to play games—well, in the words of Wolcott Gibbs, where it will all end, knows God. Hera's rage was directed precisely against a perverse and excessive revelation of truth. It is woman's secret that she is readily attracted to other men, that nothing about her sexual instinct prevents her from being charmed by certain pastoral delights like rolling in the hay. There is a touch of E. B. White's ravishing rollicking young queen bee in her:

> When the air is wine and the wind is free
> And the morning sits on the lovely lea
> And sunlight ripples on every tree,
> Then love-in-the-air is the thing for me
>   * * *
> And I wish to state that I'll *always* mate
> With whatever drone I encounter.

This is woman's secret, not to be given away by any fly-by-night Tiresias. She has had to conspire to deny this urge, to repress it in herself, to impose restraints upon all evidence that it exists, for to let herself go in this direction would be to jeopardize the life of her children, the future of the race. It would distract her ineluctably and draw her attention away from this greater necessity. And who is it that would know this better than Hera, the goddess of woman's life?

She still cannot have it both ways, it seems to me, but whether it seems so to every free and modern woman is in doubt. The human race has survived to now under the aegis of this imposing myth, but what will become of us with the imposition lifted? I must say here, that it is my experience that the centripetal forces in marriage are very strong and it would ill become me to speak lightly of their gravitational pull. If the liberation of woman from traditional expectations were an isolated phenomenon, I think the gravitational pull of family would tend to keep her monogamous, if not a hundred per cent faithful (which was never necessary). However there are other things that are nibbling at the foundations of marriage, less gay and amusing than the inherent female flightiness that has suddenly been let loose.

And there are other people besides me who are worried about the family in a more sober and scientific way. I am borrowing three points from the orderly mind of a biologist whose concern for the decline in influence and prestige of the family I ran across in *The Berkshire Eagle*. Why a biologist and not a sociologist or psychologist, I wondered at first, but since I've become a great Darwinian (by reading one book, typical) I see that a biologist would be especially alert to signs of radical environmental change as it must affect the offspring of a species, and belonging to this species he would be loath to have it become extinct. The primary reason he gives for the contraction of the family's usefulness is that God's injunction to multiply and replenish the earth has been overaccomplished.

The second reason is the present inadequacy of the family to perform its immemorial function of transmitting the culture to the new generation. It is perhaps typical of a natural scientist that in his detached and unemotional view he will see the mother as somebody of least use in preparing her boy for today's world. All the information he needs to get ahead she doesn't know. As a sample mother I can certainly testify to an ignorance that covers broad fields. Roughly anything that has followed from the discovery of electricity falls under this category, anything invented since the industrial revolution, more or less.

Black as the thing looks from the scientist's point of view, I must say it doesn't from mine, for there is a difference between understanding the transmission of power and the transmission of culture. It is like the difference between a vocational and a liberal arts education. Family life falls under art and at best the young can emerge from it with all the fine points that mark an ethical man, with a broadly exercised intelligence, with a sense of compassion and of responsibility. Where this has happened culture has been transmitted. A human being has been civilized in the best sense of the word.

Life was much simpler in a brutal grinding way under the cottage industry system when mum sat in her cottage by her distaff with her little ones around her and they all got exploited together by the new capitalist class. She had trouble getting the goat on the roof to munch the thatch (or off so that he wouldn't?), but she did not have trouble passing on the traditional moral values and making them relevant to her children. This is admittedly the crux of our difficulty. But there are several generations to account for between that sweet old lady in the cottage and me. Her children may have emigrated to America, landed sometime during the nineteenth century in Boston or New York, and surely had a terrible time making their traditional moral values relevant in turn to their own children. My grandparents, my parents, and I have all had to cope with preparing the new generation to withstand unforeseeable exigencies in an unimaginable world.

In this increasingly complicated society the cultural heritage to be transmitted needs more time in the telling. In a simpler age, when your boy or girl went off to the factory for a twelve-hour day, at 9 or 10, your suzerainty as parent came to a natural end. Now, that suzerainty ought to be extended through the better part of the second decade, and it is required, really, that you follow the parallel of a child's move into adolescence with a corresponding growth of your own, from a simple story-telling, parable-pointing mother to one who is capable of handling the subtleties of unanswerable questions. Simultaneously, the father needs to come forward as a natural reinforcement of parental authority. The mother cannot transmit culture or anything else to an independent, car-driving teen-ager who won't stay home long enough to receive it. She may look to the father for a firm hand, but she may look in vain. There is a nearly irresistible force that operates like a leak in a dike upon the confidence of the both of them. Be a little yielding and sympathetic to teen-age children, show them you are determined not to close your mind to everything they do, and on the instant and henceforth you are assumed to have an open mind to everything they do. They approach you as if they were all junior members of the Civil Liberties Union and take an open mind on any one issue as a kind of precedent which you, as the parent, are forever expected to match and even improve upon. There you are, dad, a little Hans Brinker, holding back the whole blooming sea.

Dad stands firm, holds his ground. Mum stands back, uneasy, and holds her culture. The upshot of the matter will be determined by whether their adolescent son or daughter will accept parental authority. The decline in prestige and influence of the family is cruelest here. I recall reading a short profile in the *Times* about an elderly senator from, I think, the state of Maryland, who said that when he was 18 he told his father that he thought he was old enough to have a certain freedom. "As long as your feet are under my table I'll tell you what to do," said this figure from ancient times with his shape-up-or-ship-out point of view. Can you see practically the exact same

35

thing repeated today? Only with plastic place mats and paper napkins on the kitchen table, when our young lad of say 16, brushing his hair off his pizza, announces, "I think I am old enough to ride my motorcycle without wearing a crash helmet."

"As long as your feet are under my table I'll tell you what to do," pleads and wheedles and begs the dad. Why, dad, can't you say shape up or ship out? Well, because the young today seem so liable to ship out, drift away, even without reason, without provocation, that to threaten them or dare them to go has become a little comical. How to make them stay is the problem. You give them the motorcycle with fear and trembling lest they go out and kill themselves and others, but you insist, as a matter of self-respect and a safety token that he wear a crash helmet. After a while he stops wearing the crash helmet. After a while longer he ships out, drifts off.

I cannot conclude from what I see that this second cause of the decline in prestige and influence of the family is due to the family's not being *needed* anymore for the transmission of culture because the schools and television transmit it better. It is needed, but perhaps it *can't* do the job. If it can't, nothing can in its stead. That's it.

By the time I reach the biologist's third point I begin to believe, after all, he has a bias against the family which does not become a biologist and which is why I leave him anonymous. In his words, "it is idle to talk of a society of equal opportunity as long as that society abandons its newcomers [from economically depressed homes] solely to their families for their most impressionable years. . . . Society must in effect invade the sanctity or at least usurp some prerogatives of the home if it is to assure equal opportunity for all."

Now I understand this to mean that it is the hopeless ignorance in these chronically depressed homes that condemns these children before they are even old enough for school, when no matter how enriching the curriculum, attentive the teachers, it is too late to reach them. Their capacity for intellectual growth and excitement is already atrophied. And so, you'll have to reach them earlier with public nurseries and Head Start programs. He is saying, it seems to me, that it is a cycle of *ignorance* that must be broken. I believe that in chronically depressed areas the key word is Depressed. You must break into this cycle of depression. If people have for generations lived in poverty, then hopelessness inevitably becomes a numb reflex, and listlessness will be the consequence of poor diet and unattended disease. It is the mother who is numbed physically and emotionally who cannot create in her child the essential minimum of emotional responses and reflexes. It isn't intellectual stimulation that is disastrously lacking. It is the exercise of much more basic parts of his self. He has to be handled and smiled at and yearned for and soothed from the first breath he draws. Somebody must expect and applaud and laugh at and cry over him. What has happened in the family historically, and what can only happen in the family, is the singling out of one's own infant for caring.

In chronically depressed areas there are chronically depressed people. The meaning of the term shifts depending upon whether you are talking about a place or a human being. (It shifts again if you are talking about people in the aggregate or as individuals.) If one seriously intends to revive economically such a depressed area, pump money into it, multiply the employment possibilities, I believe, in time, its population will be brought back to life too. There is a magnificent resiliency in people. We take heart, take light from one another.

This isn't to say that economic change brings a stunning reversal to every dreary statistic testifying to personal

37

failure. Wherever they test for middle class joy they come up with some terrible statistics. Still, if you are talking, in the name of equal opportunity, about the rescue of children whose faculties will not be sufficiently stimulated in such depressed circumstances then you are talking about the most intimate and early relationship of mother and child, and about troubles that won't yield to institutions provided from the outside. Head Start will work for the little fellow who toddles into it with a certain minimum emotional health, no matter if his vocabulary is very small and his experience very narrow. If he doesn't have the minimum I don't believe it can work.

What I do believe is that you can't "invade the sanctity of the home" with some sort of substitute mother. It is the mother you have to rescue. It is the family, by God (or by natural selection), that is uniquely designed to tend to all the early facets of human development.

But these things are sociological and temporal. Fundamentally, in the Advanced Society the future hangs on woman: whether her strongish urge to see her children through will enable her to evolve a suitably tough rationale in favor of marriage and family; whether it will continue to have the edge, when the air is wine, over the impulse to fly free of immemorial social restrictions as well as her own inhibitions. Or whether she will be so dazzled by pop feminist philosophy and its tinselly mod thoughts about freedom and fulfillment that she'll just pick up her marbles and walk out—on the whole human race, so to speak.

CHAPTER 3

Breaking Up the Doll's House

Whether the differences between the sexes are of cultural or of biological origin, and whatever those differences may be, they are as irrelevant to our professional, as they are valuable to our personal, lives.

BARBARA WOOTTON

Now, from that period when Hera maintained her stern surveillance over woman's life, I skip 3 or 4 thousand years and make a roundabout attempt to reach the development of modern woman through the black door. Alarm over the condition of the white American family has not, as far as I am aware, roused the United States government, but alarm over the Negro family has, and certainly deserves prior attention. This is only one instance in which my eye has been immeasurably sensitized to every shade of the human dilemma through the American Negro rebellion.

Here is the thesis, abbreviated and tailored to my purpose: that because the Negro man has been humiliated and degraded by our society for so long, the Negro family is lopsided. The father is not at its head. If he is in the house at all, he is in retreat, routed by the outside world, a figure of failure and weakness to his children. This situation perpetuates itself through the generations because the great souls among Negroes who have overcome unspeakable obstacles in order to provide their children with food and dignity have tended to be women. They, at least, have been able to find jobs. White women have had an extraordinary preference for Negro female domestic help that has been so persistent as practically to constitute a white female racial characteristic. If they had not this preference, then the Negro people since the Civil War could not have eked out existence, and some other solution to their economic problem would have materialized earlier, for better or for worse.

Meanwhile, as we know, there have been no substantial jobs for Negro men, no place of honor for them in American life. And where their women have been strong, they have made yet more lopsided the balance of powers within the family. Whether or not the mother is successful and iron-willed, the child has lacked a forceful and manly parent, and for the boy child this is a lack that is catastrophe for him. How can he measure himself? Who are his heroes? Where will he find his self-esteem? Little girls who grow up in a household without a dominant father in it are not likely to redress this imbalance when their time comes to bear a family.

It is this thesis that was presented to a White House conference to which many Civil Rights leaders were invited, and it was accompanied by the urgent warning to break into the disastrous cycle of the Negro generations. The Negro leaders listened impatiently and said, in effect, "Never mind all the psychologizing. Just provide jobs."

40

What has caught my attention in the disagreement over means is the *end*. Just whose family structure was being admired? Was it the American white family structure? Are people pretending for the moment and for the sake of throwing the plight of the Negro family into high relief, that the white family is a stable unit with a dominant father and a mother who blends in nicely and children who know where they are going?

Why the very men and women on the government's task force, who are called upon to devise plans to affect the most intimate relationships in other people's private lives, may return sheepishly to their own homes at night, uneasy lest anyone look *there* to see who is running the castle. Is the father true king, at the top of a wholesome pyramid, very masculine and authoritative, the support against which wife and children gratefully lean? Is there a round, comfortable sort of mother, content with her domestic duties, content even to be round, who gladly defers to the ultimate authority of her husband, even in the matter of rearing her young? And those children, do they all, in kindergarten, draw their family portrait in the shape of stairs, with the father at the left, very tall, complete with ten fingers and ten toes, the mother, a step lower, in a beautiful dress, and dribbling off to the right, sisters and brothers, more or less limbless?

A short while ago, not even a decade past, I believe it was generally assumed that this sort of happy hierarchy reflected the harmony the average person was part of, grew up in, the harmony that the normal American family achieved. Now we may well wonder whether, if there ever were something that could be called a normal family, just how happy all its members were. That mother sounds awful. Awful and also fat. How can a woman remain so cowlike and submissive in a world which is as provocative, stimulating, inviting as ours?

As Western civilization outgrew the primitive institution of racial slavery so has it also freed women from legal bondage to husband and father. If one could question all the fulfilled and contented and *deceased* grandmothers that are living in our memories, how many of them would assure us that their self-sacrifice to husband and children was a divine arrangement whose virtues they never doubted? How many of them might point out that self-sacrifice was the sort of adjustment you made because the legal and social laws that precluded divorce, control of property, respectable employment left you little alternative to your married situation, like it or lump it?

Still, the legal pillar that made the man superior held fast the family pyramid, and once the laws were pulled from under it, down it came. A newly freed creature will push wherever he finds give, at first tentatively and then ever more fiercely. The Negro man pushed against a most ungiving people, and shrank back; but the white woman has had the reverse experience. She has been pushing and everything is giving, and a lot of men topple easily. It is as though she has bounded loose from her childhood submission into unrestrainable adolescence and is up to the same point as her own teen-age daughter with a bursting, "I want to be happy!" "Why should I wait?" "Nobody has a right to stand in my way!" Is it fair that women should be so aggressive, so dissatisfied now that they are free? It's not fair, not Christian, not Jewish, not black or white, and it's not mature.

It is not mature of the woman in the family to feel no overriding reason to impose restraint upon herself, and when the man is badly disconcerted by her unappeasable discontentment, there evolves an imbalance in the white family which is perpetuating itself too. The great white father, routed by his wife, is not in control of his household, and his children too are lacking a strong, purposeful figure of a man by which to measure themselves, while mama sometimes makes motherhood look like a contemptible thing one gets tricked into. What is the American family portrait? Billboards around here used to carry a supersized family, pink and wholesome, pausing before a white colonial church door above the message, "Those who pray together, stay together." That was some awful pitch and surely inspired more irreverence than piety. Are our lives more accurately drawn in a pop art strip with the father alternately inside washing the dishes and outside washing the car, and the mother wondering the whole time that she is having baby after baby whether she isn't a fool not to be out working and fulfilling herself? I suppose what we really are lies in the vast between.

As the Negro man has been beaten down by society, the white man has been beaten down by the inconsolable grievances of his wife. It is not being good for the children no matter what color skin you have. Look how oddly jaded our white children are by the good life in our Great Society. It is not only the family caught in a pocket of poverty that worries about drop-outs, smash-ups, illegitimate babies, drugs. In the searching after causes why benign and generous environments produce irresponsible, indifferent, and ungrateful young, or despondent and hopeless young, the specialists point to the rootlessness from our national habit of moving and moving, to the loosening of the religious hold on us, and to the automobile which children are allowed somehow to believe is strung onto their birthright. But it is my view that these things are often peripheral and that central to all this flapping about may be a woman, breaking up the doll's house.

It is not a hundred years ago that polite society was scandalized by Ibsen's *A Doll's House*, with its accusation that Western woman was kept a child, that her emotional and intellectual growth was artificially warped by convention. Nora was the name of his heroine, a child-wife whom we watch express a slowly dawning sense of outrage over finding herself, adored wife, mother of three children, yet withal a stunted, undeveloped human being. *A Doll's House* was written in 1879, and when it opened after *Ghosts* in London, among the great majority of English critics that believed Ibsen to be "a crazy fanatic . . . not only consistently dirty, but deplorably dull," one described the people who went to his plays. "The unwomanly woman, the unsexed females, the whole army of unprepossessing cranks in petticoats . . . Educated and muck-ferreting dogs . . . They all of them—men and women alike—know that they are doing not only a nasty but an illegal thing. . . ." And what did Nora do that should put him into such a passion?

She was, when we first meet her and after eight years of marriage, still her husband's "lark twittering," his "squirrel frisking around." But then, in her naïveté about legal and other adult matters, she inadvertently brings disgrace upon her husband's name, and in the great crisis, comes to recognize, with bitterness and anger, that she has been prevented from achieving maturity, the fullness of her own development, in order to fit society's view of the Good Wife. At the end her husband says, "I would gladly work for you day and night, Nora,—bear sorrow and want for your sake. But no man sacrifices his honor even for one he loves." Nora replies, "Millions of women have done so." And then she walks out, taking only her few personal possessions and her honor, leaving her husband and children. One could not expect Victorian England to find the moral in that.

By coincidence only is our Nora Nora. Our dear friend Hermann Weigand is the author of *The Modern Ibsen,* and when he first saw her after she was born, he threw up his arms as if to say, "How witless you are!" but said instead, "Nora! Nora never grew up!" His exclamation has echoed in my mind frequently since. Nora never grew up. And today's woman hasn't grown up either, but seems to founder as if when she gained her freedom she lost her point. But she is farther along than Ibsen's Nora. His Nora was not even capable of growing up, so irremediably restricted was the development of her personality, because the fact is that the mature thing for her to have done would have been to turn round at the door and come back to pick up the pieces from the doll's house and build a proper pyramid. Otherwise, what happens to the children?

It is generations later. We can't still be in the original state of shock over how we have been kept children, how we have been denied fulfillment. We are, I suggest, beyond childhood now and have progressed to something like an adolescent state of self-absorption, more upset than ever about being unfulfilled, but no longer justifiably so.

The first Nora bolted, refusing to sacrifice herself to anyone, husband or children. She made her point. That her children were sacrificed instead was another matter then. But now we have lived with the consequences long enough to understand that the laws of nature are not abrogated by the laws for sexual equality. There are not one but two roles for which woman has been singled out, fair or not. First she must bear the child, then she must be sure that it is well reared. If this seems too much to ask, if it is Nora's self-sacrifice all over again, the mature woman can elect to remain childless. But the mature woman who does have children must know how crucial to their well-being is the understanding that the father be drawn tallest, that he is respected for his breadwinning and for his perseverance, which is sometimes heroic in the uncertain outside world. And that when he returns at night he is treated with warmth and consideration and honor. Inside the family there is no sexual equality. Boys are different from girls, mother from father, and while we, for instance, hope that our own Nora will be able to develop her mind and her character as fully as we hope this for Tony, we do not want her to become the mother who knocks down her husband and gobbles up her children. What is feminine in Nora we cherish, and what is masculine in Tony we prize as well. Why people want to overlook the charm of it all, I can't say.

Where it is true that the white man has retreated in bewilderment and guilt before his wretched spouse, the improvement in his situation must derive from her becoming, finally, all grown up. On the other hand, I don't think it is suggested that the Negro woman is immature, or that she has been obsessed by *sexual* inequality and is having trouble with feminine identification. It might, after all, be very rewarding to see what happens when you "provide jobs," to see how the Negro family shapes up after a couple of generations free from social injustice.

Suppose the Negro woman, not having been haunted by the white woman's particular grievance against men, and no longer the sole source of strength in the family, is able little by little to loosen her grasp on the household. Might she not skip the whole frantic female fulfillment exercise and come to earth in a peaceable kingdom where the irreducible difference between man and woman is not a question of legal rights but a sort of lovable law of nature? A house with babies and books in it, and a husband whose heart lifts as he comes through the door, tired from managing the bank all day, why it might not even dawn on her how unfair it is that the sexes are unequal. Future sociologists may yet look to the Negro family for the clues that would restore to health the still unresolved imbalance in the white.

46

CHAPTER 4

On Men

A woman well bred and well taught, furnished with the additional accomplishments of knowledge and behaviour, is a creature without comparison. *Her society is the emblem of sublimer enjoyments, her person is angelic, and her conversation heavenly. She is all softness and sweetness, peace, love, wit, and delight. She is every way suitable to the sublimest wish, and the man that has such a one to his portion, has nothing to do but to rejoice in her, and be thankful.*

DANIEL DEFOE

You know, there are people who are so delighted by children that it doesn't matter to them too much if they are spoiled, and that's more or less the way I feel about men. I am willing to play with the fiction that many American husbands are victimized by unsatisfied wives who are suffering from every known craving. But it is fiction; it is selective. As well to say many women are victimized by unsatisfied men. If Nora would just settle down and grow up, Helmut would come back from the bank every night to seek his peace and renewal at home, and he would find it. That is sweet. There is no place, in that lamplit hall smelling invitingly of beef stroganoff, for the father who bounds through the door, remarks in a low vicious voice that his is the only house that shines like a Christmas tree and do you know what the electric bill was last month, and spends the evening meal bullying his children with a pettiness that is laughable although nobody laughs. Nora wants a great man, but this man is *small*.

"Little man," his grandmother called him when he used to nestle in her lap, "little man." And little man he fears he has become. A boy incorporates all the sovereign attributes ascribed to maleness about the time he means to be a fireman or an astronaut. He bristles with the heroic promise of life, but as he grows up these very masculine attributes with which he must realize himself are gradually softened, redirected, emasculated. By the time he reaches adolescence he doesn't want to be a fireman any more and he doesn't know what he wants: just in some way or other to become a man among men, some sort of success. That is what it comes to, that is the residue of maleness, that is where modern man stands in the line that reaches forward from Odysseus, Philip of Macedon, Eric the Red, Richard the Lion-Hearted, Walter Raleigh, Wyatt Earp. However, it is progress.

The successful civilizing and gentling of a man is a very good thing. Were you to bump into Eric the Red or Wyatt Earp at a party you would probably come home gratified at the advances that've been made, all told. The he-man is likely to be hard, narrow, humorless, not verbal, as they say, and unless he looks as though he plans to knock you down and ravish you, not interesting. All the other men at that party were he-men when they were 5, but they have channeled their aggression into the professions, into academic life, into the wholly owned subsidiaries of international corporations. At a party men look successful. They may say, after a drink or two, that they are onto the good life, the very ones for whom life is no party.

"Who is that guy with the black velvet vest?" somebody may ask, and the answer is, he's with Hartford or Omaha, Mass General or Presbyterian, he's at California or Wisconsin, he's in oil, in electronics. A man with a glass in his hand stands for a brief moment on great territorial claims. At a party GM or GE may be shining on his shield—shield over a poor shadow. He is a shadow that began as a substantial boy, a boy who moved through high school, through college, into the company training program and has bucked his way from 20 to 40, sometimes shunted off, sometimes moved up. It has been coming to him bitterly that 40 to 60 is more bucking. With the drink in his hand, with the shield, in the velvet vest, for a couple of hours, he borrows the contentment of the good life.

Women complain of being unfulfilled. A man thinks of himself as being crushed. He is more to be pitied, she more to be censured. "I'm not having fun," she wails. But think of the things nobody asks a man: Are you having fun? Is life fulfilling? Is it fair? My mother has said (I think it was my mother) that any family man that doesn't bolt deserves a good mark.

Today the mass of men are crushed by the nearly intolerable pressures of a changing society and they were crushed in the traditional and unchanging society as well. That they lead lives of quiet desperation Thoreau noted in 1854. That we fall back upon this expression again and again is for the surpassing truth it contains. But now the pressures are different. The bright middle class boy is streamed through to middle age by such a relentless current that he cannot lift his head to take a breath, to think where he wants it to take him. Tony lifted his head

49

when he was 15, and we were worried to death lest he miss the boat. What boat? He didn't know what he wanted and where he was going, and that's why he lifted his head (if you will forgive extreme oversimplification) and we meanwhile had to say put your nose in your books and Don't Think.

My father was born in 1892 and worked his way through law school by tending bar in his father's saloon. "Why did you choose to be a lawyer?" I asked him. "I didn't choose to be a lawyer. I chose not to be a saloon keeper." That was in the heyday of the good old upward mobility movement. You probably reached young manhood then with your fair share of doubt. However, while the impulsion within you to achieve something, to go to law school, for instance, may have wavered, the impulsion to get out of the working class did not. My husband was born in 1923 into the middle class (which he has thought of fleeing from time to time) and changed his major several times during his freshman year at Harvard. He thinks of himself as having wavered, but rather in the way one wavers over a smorgasbord. What would have happened without World War II to take him off for three years and give his mind a rest, one can't say. As it was, he returned at least three years wiser and steadier, left history for pre-med, and stayed his course. The wars of the twentieth century have provided young men with a singular rest from that relentless streaming, what might be called an institutionalized break in an otherwise severely canalized life.

Tony at 17 has no sense of true vocation, and his father didn't have it at 19, as noted, and his grandfather said that after years of practice he got to love the law. If Tony could have their luck and sooner or later love the field he finally settles in, his life will be blessed, not marked by quiet desperation. Not free of it, but not notable for it.

When I think of the future for our girls it seems e
mous and gay with possibilities. But when I think a
Tony and a boy's road I sober up. I have been carefu. _
to dwell on the Vietnam war which has been going on
while I write this book and which I find repugnant, for
fear that it will not be topical by the time this is published, and for fear that it will be. Meanwhile, under its
pressure, the President asked us all to consider whether or
not college boys ought to be deferred in the draft.

Assuming a just cause, the question is, does one, by
interrupting the four years of college work, thereby inter-
rupt an intellectual process to its detriment? I can't
believe it. If there is a case for not disturbing concen-
trated intellectual work, wouldn't it rather apply to the
more mature graduate student absorbed in the continuity
of his chosen discipline?

Meanwhile, the case *for* interruption is very strong.
Tony has been in school since he was 4, and if he means to
be a lawyer like his grandfather he will be nearly 30
before he is delivered from the formal student role. In
that role, and from about seventh grade, he has been
striving, as they say, in an increasingly competitive situation. Actually, as to Tony, that is what he has not been
doing. But taking no positive notice (only negative) of his
doubts and uncertainty, we feel we must shove him along
from high school to college to graduate school, urge him
to sharpen, husband, discipline, narrow his view; and
when his mind strays we are in a flap. Why? Are we
merely wringing success out of him for our own sakes?
No. It is because we are influenced by the traditional
assumption that if he doesn't harness his mind, put
blinders to his straying eye, go straight down that track,
he'll be out of the race. A girl's life has a rhythm that lets
her wander. A boy's is a long steady gallop.

Kingman Brewster, the president of Yale, has said that

he believes it would be an excellent plan for many young people to take a break between high school and college. Their fathers before them, those that survived the great break of World War II, returned to the campus afterwards infinitely better students. They had inevitably gained a breadth of mind and a seriousness of purpose that younger boys don't have, and can't have. Some of life you just have to live through.

I have got out of the habit of believing that maturity is an absolute condition which one really ought to arrive at by the age of 21, and that if one falls clearly short of the mark it is a personal failing. Maturity is just one more woozy word roughly signifying the capacity to cope with what life is throwing at you, whenever. The problem of being immature at 40 must be almost as crippling as at 20. Meanwhile this epoch of change is too rich, too shifting, to get your bearings in it early, unless you come equipped with inherent limitations that allow you to make all judgments with simple confidence. Many do. Most of the bright young need more time, need this pause, this break, and it seems to me self-evident that a man of 20 who has deliberately taken two years off to build roads in Northern Nigeria before he begins college will arrive on the campus of a multiversity infinitely better off academically, socially, emotionally.

For the parents the headache is whether they are supporting an international drifter. It is built into our Free Enterprise mythology that if you aren't always a hundred per cent Go, you are at heart a malingerer. For the old man there is the further complication of being asked to have confidence that his boy's uncertainty, immaturity, contain the essence of certainty and maturity; and if he is paying the bills, to postpone for a couple of years the glorious day when he's paid his last.

Whenever you consider the problems of men you bump

into women, thank goodness. The next thing that comes along for a boy is the impulse to fall in love and get married, and by the revised schedule above described, it may happen to him in his freshman year. Clearly, if you tick off the traditional points, he is in no position to support a wife. But after touching on the pressures that bear down on a man in this epoch, the cheering thing that may show up is one of the best of that new phenomenon, that new breed of girl. This breed, turned out in small numbers (as yet) may be the guard advanced into that desirable maturity the absence of which I have been bewailing. This breed, by its healthy adaptation to the reality of today's world, may be the promise of human survival. This breed may not exist outside my fancy. I am mindful of the great variety of girls we are producing in this country, girls who are tempered by the many socio-economic forces of the several regions—from leftover belles in the South to leftover San Francisco hippies—but I am not a sociologist, only a mother; and drawing from my local experience with our resident girls, and projecting my hopes into their future, I must say that on average one thing could be better for a young man than it used to be, if luck is with him: a young woman.

You can team up today like a couple of equals. A sophomore—perhaps he should wait until his sophomore year—cannot ordinarily take on the expense of a little apartment, a stove and refrigerator and a bedroom suite, the addition of an unplanned baby, life insurance and a savings account, but he can take up with a girl he's in love with, marry her so that they can pool their resources, look after one another, share their growth.

Who is this girl?

Someone who is not hamstrung by the historical view that marriage is a submission/mastery equation and that in return for her surrender she may reasonably expect to be taken care of, protected, etc. Nor does she see herself as a militant female, determined to prove her equality; that would be flogging a dead mare. Instead certain aspects of equality are implicit for her; she estimates her own mind and its potential not as a woman but as a human being; and she is at peace with her body, her own sexuality. So that when she falls in love it isn't primarily for the broad shoulders against which she can rest her head, it isn't shelter and retreat she is above all seeking. The old accouterments of respectable marriage, the little cottage, proof that she has been paid in full, tend to be irrelevant.

I suppose most young women still want the cottage, but it is becoming a commonplace on the campuses now to be the other kind. This other kind and the man she chooses may feel instinctively that their intellectual maturation has miles to go and that the promises they make to themselves are not abrogated by a wedding but nurtured in their marriage. In the event, therefore, that this junior—perhaps it would be better to wait until his junior year—falls in love with a girl in The English Novel 310b, I cannot agree that they must be too young, that it will never work, provided of course, that it is a new breed bride. Let it be noted that when my own children come back in their junior years and announce their intentions to get married I will have a fit, say they are too young, plead with them to wait until they have graduated.

Now I must modify some of the generalizations I've let myself make about this bride. I only wanted to relieve the harshness of the fate of modern man by brightening it up with modern woman. It is a very happy social achievement to produce young women who are no longer defensive about their mental or sexual capacities. To the extent that it is true for each individual, to that extent does she rest on an honest base. This doesn't necessarily make her a breeze to live with. There is a generosity of nature in a man or in a woman that allows the meshing in a successful marriage, a meshing in spite of tension and along with growth. You can be liberated and realistic and not have this generous quality, God knows, neither you, a woman, nor you, a man.

Still, in an age in which women and marriage are placed under such hostile scrutiny so continuously, that men might find in them "the emblem of sublimer enjoyments" is too easily forgotten. The most equal of women can make the time-honored Goodwife; the most equal man may be solicitous and protective. It all begins, though, with a boy falling in love with a girl, and a man marrying a stranger. He binds himself unwittingly to a union that is the least simple of relationships, contains the most pain, demands the most work. Love may be killed by the shattering word, as Wilde says. And the word is the weapon, wielded the more adroitly the more articulate the couple. Marriage isn't a surer thing, certainly, for the modern young man and his modern young wife, but with the usual monumental effort, it may make a very gratifying arrangement for the long run, more interesting with a sharp girl than with a ninny. Where it doesn't work, where two strangers grow intimately offensive to one another, it is a moot point whether the chafing is more often caused by an unfulfilled woman or a crushed man.

In the event that it goes with this man as it goes with the mass of men the fault won't lie in woman's not being kept in her place. She was no picnic when she was in her place. Go backwards to the time before she had the vote, when she lacked property rights, had no sense of equality, of her total human worth, and you'll find no shortage of shrews, of destructive women. See history and literature, see Clytemnestra and Xanthippe and Emma Bovary. It is another Free Enterprise myth that you can only rise to

55

the surface by a system of displacement, by stepping firmly down on somebody else.

It is a myth that an intelligent wife has a humbling, repressive effect on a man. Quite the contrary. She can be better even than a first-rate hobby. See it this way. There is a different quality to the forces that crush a man now. In the past he was ground down by the excessive demands exacted from his society. Today, quite the other way, he is underused. The irony of recommending jobs to women who are restless and unfulfilled is that available jobs, as so many men know too well, are apt to engage too small a part of themselves. One's degree of interest and loyalty in them must satisfy the computer, and the computer is satisfied with marvelously few human qualities, a very small part of the whole human being.

If one yields to the charm of assigning a single debilitating cause to the discontents of our civilization, the cause could be boredom. Technology has relieved us from exhaustion and tuberculosis but has made us liable to this new disease, until now the exclusive affliction of the aristocracy. Boredom is endemic. It seems as if it could wipe us out. It is threaded through a man's days and years through his work and, heaven knows, through the staggering amounts of leisure time he is ever being presented with and is expected to greet with gratitude and joy: it can become the motif of his life.

At the end of *Candide*, when all the companions have settled down to peaceful farm life after a series of absolutely harrowing adventures, the old lady says, "I'd like to know which is worse, to be raped a hundred times by black pirates, to have one buttock cut off, to run the gauntlet among Bulgarians, to be whipped and hanged at an auto-da-fé, to be dissected, to be chained to an oar in a galley, to experience, in short, all the tortures we have endured, or, to stay here and do nothing?"

"It's a grand question," says Candide.

Against boredom, against the problem of leisure, there is no mass immunization thinkable, barring of course, education. (If one yields to the charm of assigning a single palliative to civilization's discontents, it is education.) Meanwhile it is like saving your soul, it is an individual fight, success depending upon constitution of mind and will, and luck in the woman a man marries.

CHAPTER 5

Reflections of an
Under Achiever

*As regards myself, at least, I am conscious of incessant
progression. At the point where I stood when I wrote
each of my books, there now stands a tolerably compact
crowd; but I myself am no longer there; I am elsewhere;
farther ahead, I hope.*

IBSEN

Now it may well be asked by what authority I speak of
men, women, and children, of monogamy, of maturity—of
maturity in particular as it came to me so late I think I
may approach it with the ardor of a convert. Was I at
least a sociology major? No. I was an Under Achiever. I
was an Under Achiever years before they thought up that
clever way of describing a student who could be doing a
good deal better than he was. What I was called was a
Constant Disappointment. I am not convinced that the
switch in nomenclature represents a clear gain on the

Phraseology Front, for I think it can be argued that the homely old words that were directed, with a sad shake of the head, toward me, carried a great wealth of meaning, implied the caring of others, reminded you, with a tug at the heartstring, how one is interlaced with other people, willy-nilly.

Now it is a long time since I have stopped being a Constant Disappointment and meanwhile I have had children of my own, and none of the girls so far seems destined to move through adolescence at the draggy pace their mother did. Already, and from where she sits in second grade, it looks like it's going to be Nora Seton, Girl Psychiatrist. She has a nurse dress and cap which she likes to wear in preparation, because she knows that a psychiatrist is a doctor, and as it is certain to be a terrible disappointment when she finds out there are no pills, no crutches, no bleeding sores, we haven't told her what kind of doctor a psychiatrist is. Each of the children, when they were growing up, found the news a blow. When, a few years ago, their father began to teach a seminar, there was a great wave of satisfied relief that swept over the children as if finally he was making a respectable living— he was a teacher, if only one night a week.

Jenny was going to be a psychiatrist, but she told me the other day that she believed she would be a naturalist instead. She had been reading Dr. Doolittle, and she noticed that he was perfectly content to shift from treating people to treating animals, and in fact was the happier for it. I don't know about Julie, but Maggie, steady old Maggie, was always going to be a psychiatrist and still is. It may seem to reflect poorly on my position in the family that they plan to become what their father is, but I must note that they all mean to write, only they don't consider writing making a living—and how true that is.

I do believe that for women in America it is a Golden

Age to be alive. But when I think of the various charms, pleasures, satisfactions in a woman's life, the possibilities I hope our girls will realize, I don't see that there is One True Way. As regards their future, someone will say that the right thing for every one of them is to Get Out of the House, and another will say the right thing is for her to Stay Home with the Children, and still another, that the only thing to do is prepare a girl as single-mindedly as you would a boy for a life's work, and a fourth will say that's a foolish waste of energy. The feminists in particular feel quite fiercely that a girl must opt early for a Lifetime Commitment.

If our girls still want to be psychiatrists when they are 18 or 20 it will suggest that they are that special sort of woman with a dominant interest to which the whole of their lives will be more or less dedicated. I say more or less because there are periods in marriage and child-rearing when the dedication is less and because, as I have said, the rhythm of a woman's life is different from a man's. But if it's still going to be Nora Seton, Girl Psychiatrist, she will have to begin preparing in college for medical school and, by the time she's finished her training, whatever she'll be, she won't be a girl.

If I try to match my own life against any of these prescribed formulae in order to see how well they are suited to be dogma, I find none of them fits. I poke out here and sag there, drift through one or the other of them for awhile but move on. It may be no wonder I take to Darwin so cheerfully because if I pass my life in review, and disregard the black parts and the hideous reverses, I can see nothing but progress and improvement. If I take a cool look at myself at 18 or 20, the years in which I would have had to fix my mind on a Field of Interest and begin mastering its rudiments, I see that I would have been in deep trouble. I could not fix my mind on anything, that was the crux of it.

I had moments of great intellectual engagement. Moments. I marvel to this day how much I picked up in the academic way, considering how unfailingly my eye followed the text of an explanation of economic determinism and my mind debated undisturbed whether I had the guts to comb peroxide into my forelock—a reflection upon the things you had to have guts for in the olden days—or should I cut bangs, or should I cut class so that I could go to the movies with Anita and Barbara and Holly and Connie. My friendships, the camaraderie I felt with a few girls at college, were so deep and nice that I still look back on that as the richest part of my life at Smith, poor Smith. The war was finishing up in Europe and girls were thrown upon each other for their amusements because there were no boys to throw themselves on. When the boys came home—by our senior year the transfer had been effected from Europe and the Pacific to Amherst—they did not really cause us to strive with more scholarly attention in whatever discipline we were horsing around in. This was true even with the couple of my friends who graduated with honors.

For myself, the whole of me was in a very fluid state. I was absorbed, fascinated by Impressionist painting and left-wing politics and men and what I was going to wear and Tolstoi and Thomas Hardy and what I was going to do after I graduated (stab of terror) and getting married (to whom?) and keeping house in a graceful, modest, intellectual way. There is this element of drift in my experience that I want to record on the theory—strange and unwarranted some might say—that it will be instructive to others. At the end of those years, the preliminary phase of my life, I ought to have achieved a certain intellectual or academic state of completion or maturation, whereas in fact I hardly achieved a beginning.

Now it might be said, on my own testimony, that my going to college at all was a total waste of the faculty time and my father's money, but the contrary is true. I am so indebted to all sorts of individuals who populated my world those four years—to many lecturers on the podium, teachers propped against their desks, who by their own warmth and learning humanized and lighted up a hundred areas of knowledge for me, that I have ever since been an unwavering supporter of the small liberal arts college. Not to be doctrinaire, I believe there is a place for the small liberal arts college in this country as I believe there is a place for a girl like me. It takes all kinds.

The kind I was could not bring the wandering mind under discipline in time to prepare for law or medicine or architecture or social work. I under-achieved to the very moment of graduation.

So there was this girl of 21, diploma finally in hand, after four years of not knowing what she liked best, of settling now here, now there, like a bee in an English garden, abruptly responsible—I thought it was abrupt—for her life and livelihood, but still directionless. Therefore, and for the purpose of stalling, she takes a fast secretarial course at the YMCA in New York City. She is crackerjack at shorthand, her first experience with being really good at something. It is 1948, and Truman has just licked Dewey, and the shorthand teacher, snuffling with sobs and running nose on this account has a hard time carrying on.

Now in a sociological way I may look like a living example of the failure of the American educational system in regard to the instruction of females. By 1950 I was married and had the first of these countless children, all that schooling, plus the Gift of Gregg, gone for naught. And as for Gregg, for naught for good.

I would not like to seem to insist that what follows has any universal application. But it was what happened to me in Northampton, Massachusetts, and to my dear friend

Frances Richardson, who lives in Richmond, Virginia, which I mention on account of Geographical Distribution: we did not grow up in the first twenty years of our lives in any way as satisfactorily to ourselves as we grew up in the second. And we found a domestic environment in some ways more congenial, in some ways a goad to finishing up the process of maturity and to continuing, by reading, in an infinitely more successful manner, one's higher education. Frances and I and some of those old Smith girls I've known through the ages, feel humble in gratitude for the dimension we have since achieved, complete with sag, from the clever young girls we were then, thin, thin in body and thin in mind.

Isn't that what we think, Frances? We're regular Renaissance women now, somewhat overripe compared to the 18-year old blue stockings at the Medici Court, but then we have this great, long life-expectancy. First we needed a house, a husband, and babies to wrap around us. *Then* we could do the hard part: grow up.

In order to find housewifery the best of all possible lives a woman doesn't have to have been a Constant Disappointment throughout school, but it is a help. Otherwise she might have ended up in law school. And then that Disappointment being of such duration, and so pervasive, it is liable to have left one, as it left me, permanently wistful about the great world of art and learning, always pulled by its magnetic force.

The other requirement, humble but handy, for success in this line of life is a taste for housekeeping. I really like the Domestic Arts. I like to cook and sew and paint and hang wallpaper. I like the purr of a baby sleeping peacefully nearby (that is the past) or being left all alone in the house when the children go to school (that is the present). I like to visit second grade on Parents' Day and see our girl sitting like a football player on a dugout bench,

63

with a dress. Come home and happily take up the
g (because I am all of a sudden crazy about spray
) and when that is finished, flop on the couch with a
good conscience and *L'Art Gothique en France,* which is
about the solution to the architectural problem of thrust,
which I couldn't even understand in English. An hour and
two pages later it is time to brace myself for the returning
hordes, talk about thrust, and the equilibrium is broken
by the dropping of green book bags, wet boots, clarinet
cases on the kitchen floor, and of cookie boxes, ice cubes,
peanut shells, orange peels on the kitchen table. It's not
all that charm-filled, this part of the afternoon, but then
all at once they're off with different friends in different
directions, except for Jenny whom I have collared for the
piano. She sits on the bench scowling, whacks at the keys
muttering, but I am reading *The Berkshire Eagle* and *The
New York Times,* and only lift my head occasionally to
say, "Keep going!"

It's not always French Gothic architecture, I can tell
you that. When I get to the end of this book, which is,
thank goodness loaded with photographs, I know I will
not go on to read more deeply in this subject. I rarely do. I
am a dilettante. And this life I describe is the life of a
dilettante, of somebody who tastes this and that, tries herself here and there, ranges without particular mastery or
discipline. Though I can testify that a bee in an English
garden can get drunk on nectar, takes some dizzy flights.
But I don't want to mock this. The learning is not disorderly. On the contrary, one comes gradually to grasp
the interconnection of all knowledge, of all art, of all the
processes and products of the human mind.

The last thing I would like to sound is smug. It was
dumb luck that got me smart, turned me from a drifty-
minded, ardent sort of girl, a terribly unfinished character, into somebody that might not be to everybody's

taste but is by comparison to me myself an unbelievable and unlooked-for improvement. Our girls, meanwhile, don't seem to be so imprecise, so sluggish in the fields of mental labor, as their mother was at their ages, and it might just be that when they are twenty they'll have a mature view of who they are and where they stand. One thing we're short of in this world is girl psychiatrists.

But should one or the other of them start getting Disappointing, should one's mind wander and her marks slip, should she fall in love and need to marry a student with fourteen more years of graduate work and no money, perhaps I won't panic. Maybe I'll think she's onto a good life, because it is hard for me to imagine a richer or more enriching thing to be than a housewife, if you are that kind of woman.

CHAPTER 6

Apprenticeship

At home, our house was rather a curious place, with all of us in different parts of it, reading.

WALLACE STEVENS

I do not mind being addressed as Mama instead of Your Highness but I don't like being called a homemaker. Homemaker, like hubby and hanky, is a word that sends a shiver through me, and it would never occur to me to call myself that. Sometimes, though, I am put into a splutter by feminist writers who insist that there is only one road for a bright girl to take, and that is the road that leads away from her front door. I said to one of these that I'd met at a party, a supremely confident journalist who rang this change to her own great profit at least, "I don't know whom you are talking about, madame, but it isn't I." "Why, Cynthia," she replied, with the assurance of a social scientist who's got his finger on your category, "you write. You are not a homemaker." "I am so a homemaker!" I bawled, but she had walked off, and my bellow filled a ghastly pause, ricocheted from the buffet table to the bar, and finished rattling hours later in my blushing head.

I run this enormous house and I rear five children and in my spare time I read a lot and I write a little to keep myself amused. But I have also made dolls' clothes before Christmas and I don't think of myself as some treacly Miss Jenny Wren out of Dickens, and after Christmas (not out of Dickens), when I am in acute need of a great visible accomplishment, I may go into one of these seventeen rooms and paper its walls. I have an unquestionable flair in this direction yet I don't call myself a paperhanger. It is, therefore, not undue modesty that has me write "housewife" down on the innumerable questionnaires that my children bring home from school, and any honest social scientist who looked at our family income would leave me in "housewife." And I am content. Now.

It is true that there are days (or was it years?) in the life of a new mother in which there is very little joy to be wrung from the monotony of endless child-tending, when the clock hands hardly move across the morning and every afternoon is three o'clock forever. It is the constant tattoo of a child's will against the mature nervous system that makes a woman mad for relief, with not much hope, but much guilt. But as static as they may feel, those first years of housewifery, they are not a static time at all, but something like an apprenticeship, a long apprenticeship. And as mine is over, I am content to flick away the past as I flick a ladybug from my wrist that would have flown off anyway. I rarely flick a day away now.

The first apprentice brought to my attention was not the one attached to a medieval guild but the apprentice of early American history, a kind of indentured slave who bought his passage from the old country with seven years of bondage to someone here. Seven years is about right. But where is it that you don't have lean years on the way to mastery of something? It is only a question for a woman, whether this is what she wants to master, and until today it seems to have been a question she might not have had the necessary detachment at the appropriate moment to ask herself. Should there be a husband in the bed, a baby in the cradle, in whatever sequence and however witlessly, then there are two human beings who have an attachment on her, and it remains for her, as I see it, to provide a refuge for the man, who almost by definition needs one, and to see that her child is cared for.

Even through the years of apprenticeship the need to care for my own children was very strong in me, and I never wished my job was something else. All I wished was that I could be alone regularly for a few daylight hours, in my own house and surrounded by a nearly total quiet with only the faintest murmurings of contentment to reach and reassure me through several thicknesses of wall. Structurally this was impossible when we lived in a Quonset hut, and it was no better really in the next house, a development ranch where the walls are cut from the same material they make loudspeakers out of.

But it isn't the lathing and plaster we have since had that has been holding me upright. I have a neighbor who shares my homely contentment and who said that when she was first married she was very serious, very intense about her domestic duties and on the day she went to the market she had to let the bed go unmade. Exactly so. For all the three years we lived in half a Quonset on the Yale Athletic Field I spring-cleaned all week long except for the day I made macaroni and cheese. When Tony was born I became a Conscientious Mother in an era when what child-rearing theories produced most of was mother-guilt.

It takes a woman time, her best years you might say, before she's brought a house to run itself, to provide comfort and order for those in residence, to reflect a little grace even. It is more complicated than learning to drive or to type, learning French or to play the piano, but there comes a similar moment of transition when the process moves from conscious application to unconscious mastery of the mechanical requirements at least. Once this metamorphosis occurs for you in driving, in typing, or in French, or at the piano, your energy is freed and you can use your head to think other thoughts entirely. That's what can happen, it seems to me, with housewifery and motherhood. After the years of apprenticeship so much can be done so well off the top of your head, while inside your mind is chasing butterflies undisturbed.

If I had a full-time job, a successful career, I would by now have become somebody else than what I am, able to dismiss with the staunchest equal righters the possibility that a housewife could be anything but wretched or dumb. But I am happy and smart. Wild horses couldn't have driven me out into the world, and they look like wild horses to me, those feminists with the flaring nostrils. They do not acknowledge the existence of temperaments like mine, the kind that yearn for hours alone in quiet. But I acknowledge temperaments like theirs. I am happy for the woman who returns every evening refreshed by a stimulating job in an adult world, ready to be wrapped around by little arms, ready to listen to piping voices. I would not have been ready. My Children for me are less an activity needing my participation, more part of the atmosphere in which I grow—as I am part of their atmosphere. I can see that the life of the working mother offers everything for somebody else, but not for me. No doubt if fate were to insist upon my wages, I would come through full of ho-ho spirit, but I would long for what I have now, and probably not secretly.

Little, however, have I accomplished through foresight. When I was a young girl and had first learned the facts of life I was completely mystified by the part in books where the young wife says, "Darling, I have the most wonderful surprise for you. We are going to have a baby," and Darling *is* surprised. He can't believe it. But I was even more surprised by their surprise. It was prophetic. Out of five children we planned one, and every time the possibility that I was pregnant preceded the certainty, I was terribly surprised. I couldn't believe it. And while my single deep sustaining satisfaction is to be home with my husband, surrounded, in a sense, by my children, a picture to satisfy the most mawkish minds, the fact remains that on rare occasions when I have caught myself in a mirror with a child in my arms I am quite taken aback by this unlikely portrait. Everybody else is used to the sight of me draped in motherhood, but I don't see me that way yet.

I don't see me that way, I see me as a sort of planet with satellites, Saturn, which Webster's says is "remarkable for its engirdling system of thin rings" (thin is not apt), otherwise identified as a "dense swarm of small solid bodies." Excellently apt. But I must point out that there is a space in the illustrations of Saturn between those bodies and itself, for I am not smothered with children and they are not swallowed by me. When I say surrounded by children I feel sufficiently surrounded when they are in other parts of the house, or even in other houses in our town.

I am not anybody's picture of ideal mother. There has been no theory on maternity written that accounts for me, even tries to explain me away. From my first pregnancy I began to follow the path out of the meadows. All liberal and enlightened mothers breast-fed their babies. All obstetricians took the pastoral view: it doesn't matter a bit whether your baby is breast-fed or bottle-fed but breast-feeding is right. I have heard it explained that this is only good medical practice to coax an infant into its mother's arms. There is Dr. Slyboots with his not oversubtle ways, no doubt satisfied against all evidence that he has resolved one more mysterious human conflict each time another reluctant mother is coerced to nurse her infant. Perhaps he is right. It may be that the women who fail to tie their newborns to them this way, and get tied by guilt instead, are fewer than I would think.

And here I see that there will be discrepancies in my testimony against those first years of motherhood. It was certainly oppressive to inhabit a nursery, the whole house a nursery, and I struggled fairly desperately to establish a few cubic feet of child-free air to escape from the demands that grind slow and fine. It is true, nonetheless, that it makes me dizzy with pleasure just to think of a baby to hold and to make laugh and to cradle in my arms. I cannot now, and never could, hear a child cry—anybodys' child—without needing to leap to comfort it. Nobody has had to coax a baby into my arms. What I've had to be told is *not* to pick it up. But I usually did anyway, and many times I've rocked and patted and nuzzled a little thing into peace, while I wept heartily myself with weariness and self-pity. It's a mixed bag.

I chose the bottle because the fact is that while five days of my intensest pleasure have been the five times I have gone into honest labor, my postpartum contentment has sprung from the total bodily separation of that baby from me. I delighted in being once more intact myself, and I delighted equally in the physical independence of this new creature of mine, that gave him an integrity that might not exist anywhere outside the state of my mind, but there it has lived.

I wouldn't push this point about breast-feeding except that the women who just adore to, in combination with the doctors who chortle approval, have spread themselves pretty heavily over the whole field of maternal goodness and virtue. This is to nudge that bovine complacency.

And if I find it useful to convert a physical preference into the intellectual cornerstone of my domestic philosophy, it may be because I need to build upon it a justification for certain repressive measures in the rearing of our children no more heartily endorsed by experts than bottle-feeding.

My initial craving for quiet never did die down, and this is a taste I share with my husband, as we have indeed shared all our deepest preferences. To begin with, we ran our household along severely democratic lines at a time when it was believed that children were coequal with their parents. As long as we outnumbered them, as long as we outweighed them even, it was democratic. After there were more of them than us it naturally became oligarchic. In any case, and with roughly parallel attention, as we admired their individual integrity, so we admired ours, and as we cared for their little needs, so we cared for our big needs.

We have always had a quiet house. Also, we must be delicately strung, for we have had a low tolerance for the sound of whining and the sight of prolonged disorder. To this end we have *im*pressed the children with our expectations, and when they stray from the rules of our commonweal, we *re*press them. If they are quiet and orderly, if they are courteous in public and behave mannerly at the table, at least as far as they are able, they have fulfilled our minimum requirements.

This is a master's voice, of course. It took the whole of my mind just to keep that first normal healthy baby alive. The assurance I have had since is from cumulative experience, what apprenticeship rewards you with, and the moment of metamorphosis was not something I anticipated as I didn't know that it would occur, or that it had. I only make it a hypothesis in gratitude. It no longer takes me a day to make macaroni and cheese and, to go back to my being Saturn, when those solid bodies need to break away, I let them.

It may be that the series of girls that came after Tony reinforced my hopes for myself. Julie, Maggie, Jenny, Nora, a houseful of scullery maids my mother thought they sounded, but in name only, we agreed. What strikes you as you hold a baby girl in your arms is that you surely don't dream of the infinite possibilities that she contains and then expect those possibilities to end abruptly in service to her own children. Tentatively I began to borrow some of her possibilities.

When I make this precious fuss about time to myself, I mostly mean to read in it. For years, through books alone I entered the great world, nor did I feel unduly restricted by not tracing the source of the Nile myself or the source of hard-core unemployment. It was a sedentary occupation, but if I needed to stretch I ironed the rest of the curtains or rooted out some children and went off with them to the market. The housework and children have been my exercise and fresh air. Had I continued to confine myself to rolling back and forth along the single track between a woman's two duties of family and house I would most likely finally have lost my balance. When I forced myself to be my own third concern, my life became tri-cornered, and what remained was to find my equilibrium within those still wobbly but certainly safer dimensions. If the whole business took seven years, it was worth seven years.

It took that time and much painful struggling for me to invest my own growth and evolution with a significance that warranted sitting on my bottom reading in broad daylight without suspecting myself of having chocolates hidden under the couch. Even today, though I do love chocolates, I can't eat them without feeling sinful. There are other signs of residual guilt, too, for I must save a pleasurable, unimproving novel to read after the children are in bed, as if while they are awake I am still on duty and what I read must be serviceable and informative.

These limitations are built into a personality, and I don't even try to overcome them. And, besides, it is fairly easy to endure interruptions, even to drop altogether what you are reading, if it is elevating and plotless, and if a child cannot be beguiled away ("Come on, Jenny," said Nora once when she was about three, "you got to lure me upstairs."), then I move from my own corner of concern to the children's with little distress.

That the children have caught the habits of reading and of liking to be by themselves is a great boon to the system. And as these solitary pursuits have been the source of my own great contentment, it is natural that I should want this blessing for my young as well. That is the mother in me.

But it is also the mother in me that is still liable to bouts of concern that our family as a whole, all seven of us, rarely participates in a Shared Experience, except that we eat dinner together, which I do not count remarkable. (And there are a couple of us who would even be willing not to share this experience.) I have been wistful about our not making a picturesque unit. I sometimes regret that we are an unsuitable cast for a nostalgic family tableau, an illustration in deep reds for December, evoking thoughts of the English gentry. The father in the faded wing chair by the fire reads aloud while his children, tastefully arranged before him, listen with Rapt Attention, and I, also tasteful, am tatting something, whatever that is.

It is somebody else's nostalgia I use because my own memory of my father's reading A Dissertation on Roast Pig to my mother and me is the sound of his "Sit down!" when I tried to slip away. Not very reluctantly have I checked off this type of Memorable Picture, along with collie and boy romping across meadow and other animal scenes, as being not congenial to the household temperament. Once when we took a stab at *The Christmas Carol,* the father of my children was yet more ruthless in his determination to reach the end of the chapter than ever my father had been. In the enforced silence we must each have told our grievances like beads, and the sulky faces so spoiled the outward effect that we never had a second sitting. I am not above faking up pictures of happy home-life for my young to reflect upon in their declining years, but I am not always successful at it.

We break off in clusters when we are in need of companionship and, except for supper and trips, we are hardly ever, as I say, all joined in one enterprise. I wonder if that is bad. Whatever else I am I cannot, by my own testimony, be admired for a self-sacrificing mother. It is a question whether the children suffer from this something that I have denied them. A fatuous question. If in those years of apprenticeship I sought my own salvation by turning toward them rather than away, would they not have long since been consumed by a woman with so large an appetite as mine?

Our Tony is still our first child. I passed last summer sitting in the front seat of our car while he drove, first with his learner's permit and then with his new license. I was the worst possible choice for that seat, but I was *available*—my only virtue. Oh, it is incredible how, in the beginning, a boy loves to drive, how many emotions are enlisted and tickled, how he experiences the essence of maleness in a nonchalance, in being stretched a little askew across the driver's seat, left elbow crooked at the open window. Look, ma, one hand.

"Tony, I'm warning you, if you don't have two hands on that wheel I'm going to . . ."

Tony is still our first child and I am bound by him to the young mother that I was, sober, inept, unhumorous,

75

critical. That's how I am when I sit in that front seat, and when I am in it too long I get worse. Sitting there, watching myself, I had plenty of time to think about the enormous and cheering changes that have taken place within me since I was 23, and also to think about the contradictory evidence of not having moved or improved an inch in some ways. Basically I have been wondering whether a young mother in our society is educable. That is to say, could she be taught to relax and enjoy her own motherhood right from the beginning?

It was a summer a few years ago that we went off one day to visit our friends the Rogers who have a summer house on a lake. There were lots of children, theirs and ours, and I had baked a cake, and after everybody had zoomed out of the car and into their bathing suits I went to get that cake and found a whole side of it nibbled away. Jenny or Nora, fourth or fifth child, I can't remember which it was, had ridden up in the back of the car with the cake. And we all thought it was so funny, so lovable, that our little toddling girl would make such a dent in the cake and think it wouldn't show. We laughed with delight about this, but I know perfectly well that, had this happened with my first child, I would have taken it as some serious breach of discipline, a lapse, a weakness in character, evidence of failure in my responsibility to mold members of the future generation. Without being conscious of how you see the thing, you look at that first child as your product, as a gauge of your mastery, a reflection of your competence. You don't do this so much later.

I am not sure whether this is a specific phenomenon of contemporary middle class America: the young wife, newly become mother, sobered and stiffened by the enormity of her responsibility, touchingly scientific in her confidence that the latest theories properly understood and applied are the right way to rear the young. She approaches her task with the zeal of an ambitious education major on a field trip, on a long field trip.

For myself, I don't wonder why I took the thing so seriously. Before I had Tony I had rarely anything to do with a baby, and had never even seen a newborn. I can think of almost nobody and nothing that could have helped me personally to relax, to take myself and my mission less seriously. Almost.

Ugh, am I glad that that self is left behind. Not entirely behind, it seems. It still turns up in the front seat when Tony is driving.

CHAPTER 7

Terms of Contentment

. . . but a sanguine temper, though forever expecting more good than occurs, does not always pay for its hopes by any proportionate depression.

Emma

As an Educated Housewife I am a member of what is probably the least pitiable persecuted minority in this country. It is a category that is even listed by government economists under Unexploited National Resources. I am regarded as a part of the seepage of useful energy that might otherwise be harnessed to jack up the sometimes draggy gross national product. Personally, I feel less like an undug mine, more in the way of a boggy swamp, useful to preserve unimproved and unexploited, for ecological reasons. But if I am a National Resource, I tell you at least I am not a Discontented National Resource.

It is one of those little awkward things, and this implies no negative judgment against Career Mothers, that there are some intelligent women, no matter how unreasonable, how wasteful the thing is, who are nest-builders by temperament. There are quite otherwise promising women who, in bearing children, really have to stick with it and rear them, as if such women were bound by some primordial need which other women more advanced in the evolutionary process had sloughed off. It is a condition beyond argument, and like the State of Grace, one cannot be talked into it or out of it. And it is consequently bouncing off the target to tell some women that they are wasting their lives at home when they ought to be out in the world living them. I am this sort of primitive Mother Rabbit as I have made plain. Don't burn me at the stake, sisters; don't throw me into the river; just fling me into the briar patch, which is the place I love best in the world.

I sometimes love it. I always feel it is where I belong, but for a few years I felt defensive about being a Happy Housewife. They were the years of the Woman Problem when it was discovered that an educated mother was unfulfilled. Now Sociological Studies have proved by research, graphs, charts, and new math that she is in fact much happier than some, and those who believe in sociology, psychology, etc. can draw comfort from this. For myself, I could never accept the essentially feminist proposition that modern woman is still the special victim of hostile, outside forces. I thought the woman problem was just one reflection of the general coming apart of the old romantic fictions we used to live by. There is hardly a social unit in America which is not followed by the word "problem." There is the teen-age problem at one end and the geriatric problem at the other. There are, in between, the Catholic, Jewish, Irish, Italian, Mexican, Portuguese, Polish, Indian problems depending upon who you are and who you think is presumptuous. And woven through all of them is what *was* the Negro Problem, but what soon distinguished itself as an essentially white problem, in fact, *the* white problem, for it indicts the moral failure of society in the United States, of Western civilization and its Judeo-Christian base.

I have watched these world problems from safe inside and there have been times, and still are, when I have very badly wanted to get out. Then it has not been a question of whether to leave the children, but with whom. For women who have not regarded every pregnancy as an unmitigated disaster—and it is only honest to say that I myself have wobbled around and out of that category more than once—for women who have not seen the trouble of a new child as something to be overcome, outwitted at all costs, the problem of leaving the children is directly related to the kind of person one could find to leave them with. And as the breaking up of the patterns of Western life has undermined the authority of every sheltering and instructive institution—family, church, school, local government—and has made even the sharpest of us incapable of delineating truth and reality, it is not illogical that this social upheaval has caused at least comparable emotional and psychological distress in people of lower economic and cultural achievement. There are no impoverished gentlewomen, no Jane Eyres, indeed no Charlotte Brontës, left over from the nineteenth century to enter our homes and with modesty, self-effacement, impeccable breeding, play surrogate mother, stimulate and guide and love our young, and all of this in French. And the other and perhaps more bitterly missed person who has disappeared is the stout-hearted, virtuous, loyal, loving, hard working, commonsensical woman, excellent to grow children with. If the moral sureness is gone in us, it is also gone in them. If we're neurotic, so are they. With their cars and their TV's to escape into, they don't need to spin their fancies around our lives, identify with us, and lucky for them, too, when the cast they have to work with is so often joyless.

So I do it myself. I even toss them a French phrase once in a while, pearls-to-swan-like. *"Amuse-toi bien,"* I call to Jenny, who's off to play. "Yop," she says. That's as bilingual as we've got, and you can see it's the English that needs the work. I bring up these children by myself and have been content to do so On Condition, on my terms. That is to say that my contentment rests upon the successful outcome of that struggle I have referred to to preserve time to myself—and I don't mean something between midnight and two in the morning—a struggle which no Outside Authority encouraged me to undertake. I have said that almost nobody and nothing could have helped me to relax, but it's not quite true. The kind of advice that was in the air then took hold of your tension and aggravated it.

In those years when I was raw beginner, no leading expert, no magazine article said: "Leave your child alone. Don't stimulate him all day long. A toddler does not make a suitable constant companion for a woman old enough to be his mother, and vice versa." Whatever I read seemed to assume a national crisis in which all over America mothers were barely resisting the impulse to abandon their babies outright, and everybody's job was to encourage them not to do it.

I don't say the impulse to abandon one's child isn't in the mother; in fact I say if it's there it ought to be cultivated. They shouldn't have kept warning me to "Watch out for darling baby!" They ought to have said, "Watch out for darling you!" I would not have abandoned Tony, but I might have forced the days to yield me more private moments with less guilt than I managed.

The overwhelming obstacle to making time for oneself is mother-guilt that clutches at you like the cramp and that is forever being aggravated by what is the latest, newest word in human development. The best thing is to forswear the subject of child psychology for ten years, even if you are a child psychologist. Particularly if you are a child psychologist. For mother-guilt becomes frighteningly distended by a diet of this stuff. And once you taste the doubt that you are doing enough for your children, why it will hang on you, as if increase of appetite must grow by what it feeds on.

Now a woman who supports the argument that to be a housewife is a demanding, draining affair begins with, "I wish, I wish I could . . . but I don't have the time." Ah, but she is the victim of a conspiracy that demands the head of the mother as the price of assuagement of guilt. It is a conspiracy among the manufacturers of Things to do For and With your children which Enrich their lives, while they take only your time and money, things which the mother believes, in her silent soul, that every other mother must be doing gladly. I will say no more about money. But we are apt to give up more time than is reasonable because we are muddled and intimidated by the psychological prescriptions that trickle down into our folk culture and simply scare us into clumsy attempts at obedience.

The most time-consuming, mind-eroding folkway of them all is chauffeuring. It's a suburban blight mostly, but one can easily become afflicted in a town like ours. I think that it is not only bad for mothers but terrible for children. It is disrespectful to them, militating against their privacy, their self-reliance. It is a patronizing and intrusive sponsorship of their activities. It is a debacle for mothers that they have rolled up the trolley tracks and stopped paying the bus drivers, for it gives little children the idea that they have to be driven some place and big children the idea that they have to drive.

The exceptions to this interdict on chauffeuring ought to be associated in children's minds with feelings of apprehension about the kind of benefit about to be conferred upon them. To buy new school shoes with good support but, alas, no pointed toes. To hear the orthodontist explain why four fine second teeth must be removed from their mouths. ("We know that prehistoric man ate a lot of sand and gravel with his raw meat and berries and this wore away a lot of Tooth Structure, and he was regularly socked in the jaw and this also wore away Tooth Structure . . .") Or else a car should promise something especially nice—a trip, a restaurant, the movies.

Now if you live in a sprawling suburb with all public transport on the fritz, many enriching and elevating things will be going on too far away for children to reach by foot or bicycle. Then you must take a long hard look at the quality of what is being offered to see whether it is really worth your time. Only a few years ago a leading social worker could say that the difference between slum children and fortune's children was unbridgeable because these latter are accustomed to the theatre, to concerts for the young, to frequent museum expeditions, from a very early age. How simple if that were the sum of the difference; and how much we have learned since. It seems a naïve view that takes no account of who the mother is, for better or for worse, as well as for richer or for poorer. And we might consider—what actually haunts my mind lately —that the young black people in the ghetto who were, presumably, not taken to museums when they were little, and who are now bursting into violence, indifferent to law and order, are, nonetheless, not indifferent to everything. They are in fact passionately angry, and it is the depth of their feelings that astonishes us. And then contrast them to many young white people, exposed to art and music from the time they could toddle, who did not thereby somehow become more deeply engaged with life, but display in their late teens and early twenties, an indifference, a shallowness or numbness of feeling, that is characterized by the very absence of passion.

To me it seems that all the taste for life and beauty you are ever likely to instill in your young will come through the everyday air they breathe in the house that bears your mark. The museums, concerts, etc. will be peripheral for children, just frosting. For some children the very quantity of enriching events actually cuts the taste.

We live in a cultural center practically perpendicular with uplift, but what my children chiefly attend with regularity is the movies, ever since somebody around here discovered it was an art form, and which are shown by our neighbor, Smith College, public invited. So when they went to see *Casablanca* I reflected that when my adolescent self sneaked off to the Loew's Paradise for the sixth time nobody in the entire Bronx nor in the whole world, I believe, saw Humphrey Bogart as a source of cultural enrichment.

Another assault upon a woman's time and mind, once she has established her house as the kind of terminus from which transportation is practically never provided, once she has become adept at fending off attacks of culture, comes in the request for trivial community service. They look at you sitting in that house being bright, and they think you are just the one to Collect for Heart. Every American community is packed like a bag of marbles with organizations and clubs, each of which rounds itself into indistinguishability as if obedient to a law of physics, with president, vice president, secretary-treasurer, program committee, and three ladies to do the refreshments. Personally, if I attend any meeting, my attention is so single-mindedly fixed upon the refreshments to follow that it is a matter of some significance to me that the chairman in charge of them should look round and cheerful.

It is first of all our sociable national temperament, our

pleasure in companionship, that causes us to join so many things, and we endure all the mechanical parliamentary procedures and the boredom out of a puritanical need to be punished before or after for pleasure sought. And the second and no less urgent reason we join is through a need to be of service to humanity, of serious use in the amelioration of some small but specific miserable human condition. Yet inevitably we become victims of that mysterious process that enlists our energies and good will only to dissipate them in a multiplicity of petty functions. We join in a burst of purpose, and then, an act of initiation almost, we are stunned into passive submission by the club.

Some people like to be group leaders and committee chairmen and make things grow bigger and signify on a national level, and they must be counted the happy few. They are too few, certainly, to fill the countless positions and offices they spawn, and here are the rest of us, at PTA's and Scouts, at ladies' auxiliaries, sisterhoods and sororities, volunteering to fill the endless empty chairs and endure hours of most unsatisfying and trivial make-work, to expiate our guilts and doubts, to substitute an empty action for no action at all. It is a form of suffering, but it isn't the kind through which you come out a better woman. It's just suffering that wears you away, depresses you, makes you feel even more purposeless than when you started.

When I attend a meeting of something it is because I've failed to stay home. If I've gotten brash over the years about not doing things conscientious mothers and fine citizens do, it all stems from my initial battle in regard to the PTA in which I overcame my better self and to which I owe countless happy hours lying on my back with a book instead of sitting on folding camp chairs in unventilated school basements listening to "Phys Ed for the First

Grade?", "Are We Ready for Reading Readiness?" and "Has the New Math a Meaning?" To all these questions, a simple No.

I don't want to undermine people whose PTA's are Meaningful. It is really very hard for me to believe, as I've read in the papers, that the John Birch Society is infiltrating the PTA, which is under a Communist takeover. I put both these outfits under public notice that they have overlooked our cell altogether, and I say this with fresh knowledge, having actually attended a meeting lately, although when I got there people did not credit me with a noble deed but said, "The only reason you're here is because Jenny is in the French performance."

That was certainly the only reason. Jenny can't pronounce "R" in any language and this makes her sound very foreign in the Vernon Street School French class, and she is much admired. People told me she was wonderful after her performance, and the president of the PTA herself thanked me for coming and said she hoped I'd be there next time, but she doubted it. Depends on if my relatives are in the program.

Julie and Maggie are in the Hawley Junior High, a remarkable institution that harbored Tony for three years without collapsing, and which I further admire for its unstated but evident accomplishment in thus far keeping parents at bay. Do you know it doesn't even have a PTA? But some people can't stand the good life, and I once received a mimeographed letter, splendid with fine citizenship and beautiful prose, lamenting the absence of this contact with our children's school and with their teachers, and listing the number of grand things we could do for them in the audiovisual way. Would we be interested in starting a PTA? Check Yes or No. It was a rare and happy moment for me.

I read an article on the PTA by an authority in the field

of education from Harvard from which I gathered that the tendency in this organization to be a meaningless bore appears to be nationwide and insurmountable. In our neighborhood, which is chock-full of faculty wives and other responsible types, the PTA programs dash madly between How to Use Your Public Library and Safety First for Our Children, dashing, I remind you, without me. The Harvard man says that it is an exclusively middle class outfit, rarely attempting to lure the underprivileged parents, rarely discovering the challenge of enriching the deprived. A bunch of lily-gilders. He says that the reason the parents of Less Fortunate children do not turn up at the PTA is that they feel frozen out by the gentility. They are lucky.

Put it another way and you might say the Less Fortunate parents are More Fortunate, at least in this case, for understanding immediately that the long and boring PTA program is going to be long and boring, and so they don't go. And as there is nothing in these meetings in the social-climbing way that is very useful, they stay home and watch TV and get credited once again with No Motivation.

Meanwhile anybody interested in Reading Readiness, for instance, could hardly avoid noticing the unending supply of magazine articles on this subject and could bolt down a considerable range of opinions in his own living room while his betters were wriggling uncomfortably in the school basement. Personally, I don't think it is over-promising in an adult to find Reading Readiness all that fascinating, considering how full the world is of a number of things.

The awful waste about the PTA is that there is so much it could be doing, so much that needs to be taken in hand by interested parents of a community. If the proposed PTA in the Hawley Junior High were to discuss Ways of

Solidifying Opposition to Teenagers, if it merely gave itself over to jacking up morale of parents, inspired them with the courage to go on . . .

I used to think there was some larger purpose served by my turning up faithfully, something larger, that is, than having one of my children's grades win the parent–attendance banner. There has been no evidence to support this possibility. I once passed two hours aghast over a fairly heated discussion of what the optimum number of record players for our elementary school might be. I foresee an infinite number of such arguments raging in the proposed junior high PTA, dealing as it will, with a much larger Physical Plant, and I foresee my not being there to hear them.

My mother never went to the PTA. When I asked her why, she told me that she was too old to be going to school, and I was left with a comfortable feeling about this, and indeed about almost everything concerning her, that she did not travel with the herd because she was beyond it. Above all things that I owe to her is this illusion that she lived life on her terms, and I believed this unshakably until long after I was grown. This illusion was the chief reality of my childhood and deposited in my soul the certainty that it could be done: you could live life on your own terms, and indeed you must; that is your goal.

I must return to this question of enriching children's lives. If I seem breezily to have dismissed museums and concerts for them, it is once more the master's voice. The girls are mad about art and music, about wandering through French cathedrals and English abbeys. Even Nora. And I see how it's done. And I see it is to their father's credit that they are at home and in love with all that. It was he, when we were younger, who was the great bottleneck to my pouring culture over the children, who resisted being included in any family improvement scheme I had in hand, who, if I interpreted his words ("Absolutely Not!") correctly, didn't want me ever to plan anything that included a ticket for him. He suspected me of always hoping that he too would derive pleasure and even enlightenment from some Good Thing we would do with the children. This he would not derive.

He would not do something cultural *for* the children. Later, when there were so many of them that we couldn't leave them behind, he allowed them to accompany him to see the pictures and even the countries he wanted to see, on sufferance, contingent upon their perfect behavior. And they, out of gratitude (?), instantly loved what he loved. But until then, the number of cultural events we took in annually *en famille* was one.

Just when Julie's birthday came around the Amherst College Theatre Department put on a Shakespeare play, and the children, not then suffering from overexposure in the culture line, God knows, took on Shakespeare with unlikely ardor. I remember Maggie's sitting by the kitchen table, reading Lamb's *Macbeth* out loud with an intensity of interest that humbled her mother. When she finished she lifted that open, honest face with the great wide eyes and the overlapping teeth, and she said, "I love to go to a Shakespeare play. I used to worry about there not being refreshments but now I don't care any more."

Our most memorable Family Night was our going to *King Lear* when Julie was 12. *King Lear* has to do with a terrible lot of human frailty in one aged, ailing father who makes rash, foolish, arbitrary judgments on his daughters. "Lear only had three daughters to suffer from," said our own father with a sympathetic sob, failing foolishly to take a wider view.

If you think he learned from Lear's experience he didn't. He dreams of a long, golden old age attended by four solicitous, self-effacing daughters, puffing his pillows quietly, uncorking his wine gently, sautéing his supper exquisitely. Where they would be likely to pick up that self-effacement, I can't think. It does seem odd that he should anticipate a covey of Cordelias when, if there is anything at all to the law of cause and effect, he might better be laying things away against Regans and Gonerils.

The fact is, he has his own daughters buffaloed. They think he is the best possible father, credit him with every kind of superiority, and it was Julie who many years ago made it clear how things stand with them. She must have been in the third grade, and she was Mary in the Christmas play, and the audience of parents was conspicuous, as it always is in our neighborhood grade school, for the quantity of fathers it drew.

Now I know that this was merely a reflection of the Role of the Father in the American middle class family, but it is a role that has always been written differently in our life. For us it's a part from some other play—*Lear*, possibly, as noted. In any case, it has been clear to the girls and to Tony, too, that their father does not go to the PTA because he doesn't like to go, but that he cannot go to the Christmas plays because he has to work. Nobody has ever thought a thing about it.

Except Julie. We were pouring out of the school that morning after the play, great quantities of mamas, papas, children, and Julie tugged my arm to bring me down to her whisper, and she said, "I'm awfully proud that you picked your husband to be our father, do you know why? Because he is the only father that is too important to come to school."

CHAPTER 8

On Being Your Age

The youth of America is its oldest tradition. It has been going on for 300 years.

OSCAR WILDE

It seems to me that illusions with a touch of Promethean promise are very good to have embedded in the tissues of a child, and if he moves with relative success through a long life he may never to the very end have quite got rid of these illusions. They may account for his success. I had the illusion that my mother set the conditions for her life, that she made life yield her contentment, that this was possible. I had the second illusion about her that she was ageless, neither young nor old, and that she was a beautiful woman. Indeed she was an exceptionally beautiful woman and still is as she approaches 70. But the ease with which it seemed to me she moved through the decades of her life, never struggling with a sense of lost youth, never attempting to stop or disguise those celebrated ravages of time—that ease, she tells me, she didn't have. Forty was a body blow.

The dimension of time in the life of a modern woman

wears two masks like the theatrical masks of classical antiquity. The tragic mask, which was ferocious rather than mournful, may represent the slow passage of time necessary for healthy organic growth, or for the maturing through adolescence of the human personality, or for the long apprenticeship as housewife. This time cannot be jumped. How slowly pass some of the years of your children's childhood. How its pace may make the young frantic and frustrated. But there is nothing to do about it. This mask of time is ferocious.

The comic mask, which was not so much funny or happy as maniacal, is time being swift, and it seems that time suddenly, abruptly switches masks, assumes this terrible grimace, as you approach your fortieth birthday. I have just successfully negotiated that hairpin turn, a success, I must emphasize, I owe in no small part to the illusion that my mother moved with easy elegant dignity through the stages of her life, and that it seemed less perilous to look your age than to look a fool.

I did find that approaching 40 really occupied the mind. How somebody so young could be so old. I had always felt that people are more or less the same age that I am. As a child, it seemed to me that there were mostly children in the world. When I was 25, it was what one more or less was. In my early 30's I felt vaguely that I was in some sort of population swell. Now that I am 40 I console myself with the idea that so is everybody else. Sometimes it's hard to believe. When I walk across the Smith campus I am occasionally assailed by doubt.

There were a thousand little decisions relating to the great problem of how best to pull off being 40. When I finally turned up at that PTA last fall and I let my eyes travel over the heads of my fellow female parents, I discovered that, not counting grandmothers, I was practically the only one being gray.

I had heretofore had my head dunked in a dye pot and kept myself ageless for about two years. The color was She-Does Brown, popular with horses, and as I didn't seem able to manage anything more subtle, and as I saw this picture of a very beautiful, very rich young woman with gray hair in a magazine . . . But I don't feel steady about my decision. I cut my own hair, and I find I must restrain the urge to chop deep into where the gray is thickest lest I pierce the skull. And on top of having to persuade myself how lovely it is to be gray is how handsome it is to be fat. Gray and fat. I am always looking around for moral support, and sayings I collect are like the one I saw in *The Berkshire Eagle* from a New York coiffeur who was visiting Pittsfield and was quoted as saying, "The youth bit in this country has gone all out of proportion. A woman doesn't start to become beautiful until she gets older—her whole carriage, facial expression, the eyes improve with age and attitude."

I spent the whole of last year getting ready for this birthday, fighting decay of mind and body. Nora was in school and, after fifteen years of my being half drowned in children, they all abandoned me. I didn't think I would suffer the painful adjustment once everybody was in school that other women report, because I had such a backlog of things I wanted to do. Only I didn't want to do them. I wanted to take up sewing again and make everybody printed quilted jumpers the way my friend Priscilla did, because sewing isn't fattening, and I wanted to read French history and the Lake Poets, and if it had turned out I was going to have another baby I would have fussed and carried on something terrible and taken the idiot box out of the television room and put up new wallpaper and painted the crib. Outside forces would have stepped into my life once more and committed me to a round of familiar activities which are unceasing, outrageous, and dear, and let me once more yearn for the day I would be free.

It was not only that my spirits were adroop—(I find to the question, "What's the matter with you now?" that by having the soul afflicted, rather than the body, you cut off those who say, "Take an aspirin.")—but I also had Physical Symptoms. It was therefore fortuitous that we took off in the spring for Washington to visit some of my relatives. It was a successful trip not only culturally but medically —medically because it offered me the all too rare opportunity to compare my practically unheard of ailments (practically unlistened to, would be closer to the truth) with members of the same blood stream, you might say. Things do run in families, and I know that the Russian royalty had problems about bleeding to death long before Darwin was born.

In Washington, when my cousin Frances' husband said he was married to the world's worst hypochondriac, my husband gave him a Derisory Look. This cousin of mine is really great. She had already been 40 for some time, two or three years at least, but she seemed very young and handsome and healthy. But she was not, she assured me. She is in the habit of rapping herself about three inches below the esophagus in the general vicinity beneath which she believes flourishes her decay and shouting, "Dorian Gray! I'm rotting from the inside out!"

While I was in Washington I limped a good deal, sometimes even pressing my hand over my right hip bone, always maintaining a brave expression on my face, waiting for somebody to say, "Cynthia, what's the matter with your hip?" Nobody said it. Finally I asked Frances to say it.

"Cynthia, what's the matter with your hip?" she asked feelingly.

"Sinus," I said.

"Sinus? In your hip?"

94

"I'm riddled."

"That's what I must have!" she cried with happiness.

That's why I think it is a good idea for families to keep in touch.

When we got home again my husband added a third response to his repertoire. Alternating with "Take an aspirin" and "Everybody has something," he began to say, "Why don't you go to a doctor?" And that was what I was preparing to do. I had even begun a list so that, when I was facing the doctor nervously in the office, I could remember to tell him everything. And a map. I put up the list on the bulletin board in the kitchen, but people around here are so careless. When I went to add "diet" to "right hip" I already found underneath "kosher pickles, chunky peanut butter, chocolate chips."

I had been on the kind of a diet where you can eat all the celery you want. This diet was certainly important to remember in my Health History, something the doctor could note in answer to the question whether there had been any change in my pattern of living lately. Otherwise he might never think of celery poisoning, for instance.

But I didn't go. I must have lost the list at the market, and one day when I wasn't thinking, the sinus moved right out of me. One day I lifted my head and thought: I have never felt better in my life. Maybe I am in a quiescent period, to further draw upon and distort Darwin. There are eons in geology when nothing is being deposited and nothing is being worn away. I certainly hope I am in such an eon. I am now not only willing to give being 40 another year, but more than that, I am affecting a great admiration for the subtler pleasures of this middle period. Youth, get-up-and-go, technological improvement, a high gross national product—how others love and admire it all! You don't hear much about the pleasure of being a little passé.

This country and everybody in it is so single-mindedly

possessed by the idea of eternal youth, it's a regular Ponce de León complex. As much as can be said for it as a way of egging on people under 20 to be achievement oriented, it is no preparation for the later years. There you are in the later years, foolishly regretful over what you might have been instead of calming down and gently breathing in the charm of being overripe. This is exceptionally good advice for those who found that to be young was not very heaven.

A touch faded is what I am and what I recommend. My husband has always been taken with the story of the lover who had a single rose, one day past the height of its bloom, delivered to his *mature* mistress each morning. Not that I have ever gotten a single rose of whatever age and condition—of the rose or me—delivered to this house. It's just a nice story about being faded, is all.

In America, to look a couple of years younger than you actually are is not only an achievement for which you are to be congratulated, it is patriotic. It is an example of a fetish of an idea that sways the national mind against reason, the least worrisome example that I can think of. We can see that it's commercially clever to sell the proposition that each of us can buy a few more years of youth, of life. It has such a big market. The young are presumed to be charmed—not glutted, not bored, but charmed—by this unearned attention, and the rest of us are either beguiled or intimidated. But there is nothing inherently bankrupt in the contrary proposition that age brings dignity, assurance, detachment, humor, and that effort is better spent bringing all this stuff out. I hesitate to push the delights of gradual decay, as it quite obviously is a self-serving ploy and otherwise may appear trivial. In terms of the world's crises it is trivial, but in terms of the individual woman moving through the thirties it is significant for the fifty years of life she may yet have to live through. How does she see herself? And how does she want to be seen?

Bernard Shaw's epigram about youth being wasted on the young now seems to me Edwardian, premodern. It sounds a little naughty, something you'd deliver with a wink, as if to say, now that I am so clever I would like to take a first-class fling at being young. We don't wink at anything any more—no need—and if you want to be naughty you only have until your sixth birthday to be it in. But one of the sweet wonders of our era is that you can take a first-class fling at being your own age. You can be handsome, feel fine, and look thirty at thirty, forty at forty, fifty at fifty, up to the end, in fact. There's room for us all. There's room.

CHAPTER 9

On Becoming a Mother-in-Law

Grow old along with me!
The best is yet to be
The last of life, for which the first was made.
ROBERT BROWNING

Many people may doubt that one can hang on, looking more or less grand, to the last of life. I even doubt it, no matter how much I read what I say. Furthermore, it has somehow come to pass that the last of life will be the best only by the rarest chance. To grow old now, a century of Progress having scudded by since Browning, is to become ill and feeble and lonely and frightened and not die. But if one is in the wide midway between that and actual youth itself, there are other things to think about.

Let us accept the American woman in all her youthfulness. She has the longest girlhood in recorded history. She begins to be of an uncertain age about the time she enters high school and can, with imperishable ardor, reach the end of a long life, still of an uncertain age. It is the Dorian Gray syndrome we all share: deterioration is proceeding apace somewhere, but not on the outside, as long as we can help it. I, for instance, should be worn out from childbirth, fat from overeating, gray from the course of nature, and getting ready to lay down the hardest of life's burdens and rest through my declining years, respected and loved by my children and grandchildren. But I am not worn out by childbirth now—I was but it passed—and the gray, well I've mentioned my scuffle with the gray. I sincerely regret that we do not live in a culture where to be beautiful is to be fat and everybody eats as much as she can.

Yet however coy I might want to be about my age, there are Tony and Julie, both already bigger than I am. The fact is I am closer to grandmama than to graduation day. Though I am sheltering myself from the winds of change, the children are breezing along, and one of these years, in spite of my most absurdly youthful poses, I'm going to find myself a mother-in-law. I have therefore begun not to skip those particular How To articles in the magazines of the waiting rooms of whatever I am waiting for.

It was *Redbook* that transcribed the discussions of two little forums, one in which mothers-in-law talked about being mothers-in-law, the other in which daughters-in-law talked about being daughters-in-law, and in each case the mediator, or perhaps it would be better to say, the informed mind, was Bruno Bettelheim, a most gifted psychiatrist of unusual insight, and author of *The Informed Heart*. As I read along I felt an unaccustomed sense of compassion and understanding for the mothers-in-law who were all of them so firmly rebuffed by the young, and so justly aggrieved. I had it for them, and curiously, I had it for myself. Because if it has become, in today's America, a relationship practically guaranteed to be ill-joined, why then I can see that, where I have failed to be satisfactory to my own mother as well as to my mother-in-law, it is not altogether an indictment of my character but the fault once more of changing social forces that have been creating in rapid order a series of desirable female images against which one is always nervously measuring oneself. The female image of the moment is like the hemline of the moment, something you say, impatiently, that you will not be a slave to, but you are intimidated anyhow. Your eye goes over to the enemy and you find yourself taken by the new look. Mother, daughter, mother-in-law, grandmother, wherever you are in the continuum you do not feel that time is the great help it's supposed to be, that time mellows anything, that time makes any of you appreciably more tolerant or congenial.

The role of mother-in-law has always had something foolish about it, has always been mocked. But today it is more complicated, harder, as every relationship is today.

Meanwhile the tension between mother-in-law and daughter-in-law is an absorbing topic for someone who is one and on the verge of the other. Letting myself feel a sort of hybrid of the two I found, as I read on in *Redbook*, that I veered off in a tangent, away from Dr. Bettelheim's plea to bring greater honesty and self-examination to the confrontation between the two women—away, in fact, from confrontation itself. Salvation for me, and for every woman whose foolish son is going to bring home some wildly inadequate child bride, is to use my (still) alert mind to divert my extraordinary (for my age) energy toward something else besides my married children. The problem of how to behave as a mother-in-law is likely to be just as large as the time your mind gives to it. It seems to be a common condition among the females of a family that by watching carefully, any one of them will prove herself a veritable manufactory of grievances. By not watching, you fail to notice how regularly your feelings are being overlooked.

I know that a new bride and a new household will dangle like a lure before me, and that when a new grandchild comes I will naturally want to gobble him up. This will be, according to Dr. Bettelheim, the reflection of the need of an older woman to recapture her own young motherhood by cradling her grandbabies. Perhaps this resurgent longing to replay one's younger role may be something new in woman's history due to the circumstances of modern living: the mixed blessings of leisure and practically perennial youth. Whether it is new or old, it is not a longing a modern woman can afford to be obsessed by. I wonder whether we aren't misled by the romantic mist, rising like steam from the set tub, that hovers over our view of family life in the good old days. Why should we assume, looking back to the time three generations remained under the same roof, that the younger wife and the older performed their distaff duties harmoniously, went their appointed rounds in most amicable and unlikely agreement? How many of these extended families, as they are called, shared instead a little crooked life and lived all together in a little crooked house?

In any case the older lady must have been very *tired*. She had probably borne a large number of children, reared as many as lived, was regularly overworked and broken hearted, and it is hard to see her wanting to recapture a process that must have already seemed interminable. My own grandmother was tired and passed the last decade of her life pretty quietly, and though I believed she loved me it never crossed my mind that her not seeing me more often was some sort of deprivation for her. It doesn't cross it yet.

My grandmother's lot is not likely to be mine. I was a little weary, but now I am in pretty good shape. It is still open to me to rinse those silver threads with Living Color. In such excellent condition as this, how can I see myself as an august matriarch, the proper object of great respect and little services? My daughter-in-law, who will surely be uneasy enough about her own new role, may well be flabbergasted by me in mine.

For I, as mother-in-law, will have had all the dignity and significance written out of my position by the present unsentimental progress of social history. Free baby-sitter could sum me up. (But I may charge.) Were I the very font of wisdom, the richest repository of cultural tradition, and that son's wife the emptiest vessel, I would toss her even the least crumb at my peril. A red line has been drawn through my usefulness by, in Dr. Bettelheim's words, "the stated philosophy of this country, with its emphasis on individuality and on children striking out on their own." Will she learn to cook? She can cook if she can read. Will she misrear my grandchild? No worse than I its father. The consequences to the young woman who denies herself access to me, cultural wellspring, may or may not be significant, but they will remain unmeasured.

Reflecting upon what is new between these ancient adversaries, Dr. Bettelheim notes that "no customs have yet developed for mother-in-law/daughter-in-law relations when both are fully active in life and when the age difference is too small for the one to command tacit respect and the other to yield it without misgivings." All of us, young and old, are uneasy about our place and our meaning in this modern world. The young girl is absorbed entirely in establishing her own identity and will have few clues as to who I am. Who will I be? If we are both bouffant on the top, bermudas on the bottom, will I not be miscast? Were I to look into a glass lightly, would I not remind myself of the ten-year-old Miss Ninetta Crummles, Infant Phenomenon from *Nicholas Nickleby,* who had been "precisely the same age—not perhaps to the full extent of the memory of the oldest inhabitant . . . "? The young girl who greets me in this disguise of contemporary, of friend, may very well be confounded in her esteem and estimation for I won't be 20, won't have the tastes, interests, judgments of 20. We will have no customs to guide us here, no dress to distinguish us, and as a friend of mine once said about her mother-in-law, "I *can't* call her Mrs. Jones, and I *can't* call her Mary, and I *can't* call her Mother; so I don't call her anything." Awkward, with a lot of conversation beginning with "Ur . . . um . . ."

Yet it is not that the mother-in-law is an ogre but that she is in an ogerish position. The mothers-in-law taken on by Dr. Bettelheim certainly did not sound like redoubtable dowagers storming fortresses, implacable in the exercise of their historic prerogatives. They seemed, in fact, exhausted from being tactful and understanding, and they felt as though they were forever walking on eggs. And in back of all they said was the sound of their own younger selves and the pain and shame they had experienced in relation to their own mothers-in-law. (Or so I heard.) What is unfair is that their restraint and tact are never registered to their credit. It doesn't seem to matter if they speak out or keep their mouths shut; they're damned if they do and they're damned if they don't.

When I remember myself as a child, I don't look very far into the past; and to imagine my own grandchildren, I don't look very far into the future. Little girl, young wife, mother-in-law, I am all of a piece, but the most vulnerable time, the years of my most acute self-consciousness, were the first years of marriage. That younger woman has put a stamp on my life. For that self I have sympathy, distaste, affection, and am relieved beyond measure that whatever else I may become it won't be her again. This may be the reason why, close as I am drawing to the older woman's plight, I remain on the younger's side.

In America girls are brought up on the belief that there is only one woman to a household, that upon her marriage a woman "strikes out on her own." From her wedding day she is a fortress of independence and from that moment is excessively sensitive to the tactics of her husband's mother who, being fairly up-to-date, is not likely to storm so much as to infiltrate. Soon we take on motherhood and with such a wealth of self-doubt that we simply cannot afford to have any of this doubt confirmed by somebody else. Our friends and contemporaries do not go around doubting us because, probably, they have themselves to doubt. But one's mother-in-law has a mind free for this, and she is in the singular relationship to you that allows her to doubt away. When she walks through the door of your house, it becomes a house of cards, a thing so tenuously balanced that should she wipe a nose or wipe a dish the whole of it could topple down.

What sort of attitude can I, as mother-in-law, take to a girl like that? Clasp her to my bosom, love her like a daughter, do things for her, or, on the other hand, collapse on her doormat and let me be her problem? She is as prepared to love me as she would an exposed flank. We will both be weighted down by the historic lore of love and mutual need, and she will bear the greater guilt for not loving me instantly and not needing me at all, and I will be left with the pain of not being loved and not being needed. Well, I know already that I will not be needed, and Dr. Bettelheim's grandmothers knew they weren't needed from their intimate experience of not needing their own mothers-in-law. Some of this is not a new story any more, and, although it is a modern condition has still been with us for a few generations.

You could say that a modern woman has two lives, distinguishing her from a cat. Once she has grown up the lives begin to run concurrently, which may sound like a prison sentence and which feels like a prison sentence to many. If being housewife and mother shouldn't use up one's younger years, once you've caught on, being grand-mama won't fill up the later years fruitfully either. If, as Dr. Bettelheim points out, new customs have yet to be developed for mother-in-law/daughter-in-law relations, they will have to be preceded by the development of new customs in the rearing of little girls. A little girl must learn that she has these two lives ahead of her, learn it with joy, and prepare at least psychologically for both. By the time she herself becomes a mother-in-law that second life should have become the absorbing one so that she might have to steal the time to greet her new daughter-in-law, hug her new grandbaby, pleasures sweeter for being stolen. It follows that the focus on the relation between the women of two generations is deflected because the full force of the older woman's interests and needs has gone off in a different direction. What both women are spared is the insistent and prolonged confrontation that can spawn endless bitterness and jealousy.

I do not agree with Dr. Bettelheim that more honest self-examination, more open confrontation between the two women will go some distance toward an improved relationship. Both have too much life and energy to meet head on. I think there is something to be said for moving toward each other sideways like crabs, hesitantly, the way you move into friendships. For the older woman, and here I feel suddenly all the vulnerability and poignancy of her position, the caring and loving at stake is enormous, and in this world of new relationships a new kind of delicacy is needed for it.

As I am sure to be clumsy at delicacy my own hope is that I will take my perennial youth and my unexhausted energy and go find the number of things the world is so full of. And when those little ones watch me whoosh off and ask, "Where is grandma going *now?*" their mama will say, "Impossible to tell. She makes Mary Poppins look earthbound."

CHAPTER 10

For Engagement and Against Withdrawal

"God is dead" is, strictly speaking, no more than a meta-phorical way of saying that people have ceased to believe in an illusion. In this sense, "God is dead" means, quite undramatically, that God never existed and, if so, nothing has changed in the external universe. The world is as it always was, a changing set of phenomena that human beings see from a given angle and have to cope with as best they can. Nothing is any more, or any less, permissible than before. No doubt all human minds begin by looking for an absolute, but if there is no absolute to be found it is surely immature to go on feeling indignation and resentment at its absence. It is one thing to suffer from Existentialist vertigo, which is a basic state of not-knowing from which everybody starts and to which everybody returns; it is quite a different thing to escape form this vertigo by turning it into hostility against other people or against a non-existent deity . . .

Clearly if the world is not to end with a series of

psychological bangs before the one big bang, we need
some sort of mental hygiene for a godless universe.

JOHN WEIGHTMAN

When Julie was about 10 she said, "Do you know, mother, that we are an odd family to grow up in? We haven't a religion and we don't believe in teen-agers." Well, that's not true any more. I do believe in teen-agers. I clap my hands—when I don't smite my forehead—and say that they are really true. I did make a fuss in the beginning, did not want to be the mother of adolescents, had to be hauled, tearful and protesting, into this role, but now that I've played it for a while I find that I want to explore my fascination with that bizarre and alien society. This requires the most intimate look at myself, more so than for other sorties I've made into our personal life, the past as young wife and mother, the future as grandmama. This one glances into the permanent present, and will glance off and not into the tentative signs of success and failure my children feel in themselves, feel us to have been as parents. Real pain I am going to spare them and therefore spare me.

I now think, regretfully, that, when an adolescent breaks away, if he doesn't hurt you his break will be of no use to him. It is ancient wisdom and modern psychology that he must separate himself in order to establish his own integrity, and this is the process we call rebellion. But somebody has asked the question, about the behavior of the young in our era, whether it represents rebellion or schism. And I wonder whether there is not a change in quality between the ordinary traditional rebellion, which presupposes an eventual resolution, and the cool drift of many of the children I know, along with those who "make the media." Is there a difference in kind? How could it be otherwise, emerging as they do from an environment in such radical upheaval?

I thought the way they listened to their music corresponded to the way I bought Benny Goodman records and wore out "Old Black Magic" and "As Time Goes By." But now I believe that music for them is infinitely more pervasive, wraps their minds in a membrane of rhythm that muffles the adult world. In the beginning, when this stuff invaded our house, I was frightened. It seemed like a drug that dulled the fine edges of thought so that when you read and did your homework you were prevented from having those rare moments of deep penetration by this caul or tissue of sound. I don't think I am wrong now, so much as I have come to believe that this music has a content and ramifications that ours never had, and that this protective tissue of sound may be taking the place of the protective tissue of Belief that remained safely unquestioned by all but the rarest of children through youthful rebellions of the past.

I am referring to a composite belief that includes a belief in God, a belief in the American destiny, in chastity before marriage, and add what you will. There have always been individual unbelievers. What is different now is that the invitation to disbelieve is extended so widely and so breezily, and that the young are readily but unselectively accepting this invitation, trying it out and finding that it doesn't hurt. (It does hurt.) It is spread so wide through the marvels of electronics, those same marvels that make them feel America is filled up to the top with cant, the same marvels that fill it up.

Our family may be atypical to some degree because we never had any religion, but so far from wanting to pummel anybody with my own unbelief, I must note that religion, Judeo-Christian morality and ethics, fascinate me. I cannot let them alone. They are as much the quarry for me, when I am searching something through, as they are for my friend Jean, for whom church and religion are very important. She told me when her son was 14 and preparing for his confirmation that he began to protest against taking this step, that he had reservations. "You'd have to be an idiot not to have reservations," she told him. Essentially, we are all trying to say to our adolescent children that the things we admire, the traditions we love, are really extremely interesting and worth cherishing, if they will forbear, be a little tolerant. But at 14 a boy or girl seems to slip suddenly, swiftly, out of childhood and sideways through a thick, clear glass, where we can see him plainly, and he doesn't hear a word we say. He hears that music and he hears the variants of one idea: the grown-up world is a cause of grief.

He moves through the glass into a kind of gay, chintzy bazaar, to use a physical image, where every variety of ware is being hawked, hot rods to flowers to drugs to brocaded vests and purple hair dye (and one cannot foretell what will be next), in the open air thick with their special sounds—Beatles, Baez, bells—and in this bazaar he roams about, in and out, for a long time, for several years, sampling a wide range of joys and despair. Then I see him moving along, finally, into the rest of his life, by one of two roads, engagement or withdrawal.

I am a parent and not a philosopher, and I therefore see engagement with life as success, roughly speaking, and withdrawal as failure. It is, of course, obvious that I cannot be talking about millions and millions of young people, for the mass of them are not, for better or for worse, seriously drawn by the seductions at either end of the continuum, neither by the wiles of hippiedom nor by the Peace Corps in the wilds of Africa. I am talking in particular about the withdrawal, or better, the irony in the withdrawal from life of so many of what I will again call fortune's children.

It reminds me of the generational pattern, that is either true or apocryphal, concerning the children of American robber barons, that despite the enormity of their wealth they were despondent and even suicidal, disproportionately so, that is. Those American children today, having the great good fortune to be born into intellectually stimulating families where truth and beauty are the household goddesses, and where freedom from superstition and traditional mythical warnings is remarkable, these children, who ought to be the most vibrant and exciting and promising of human beings, so many of them seem to have turned on, slipped off, opted out. A chemical or psychological numbness is their characteristic. Never in the history of good parental intentions do so many failures seem to have taken place.

Now this opting out is justified by the conviction that our society is venal and brutal and self-deluded, and I believe it. I also believe that to put flowers in your hair like poor mad Ophelia, and to smile impassively and love indiscriminately, is a charming rebuff to orthodox expectations, but it is thin, and short-lived, and immensely selfish. What offends me is not that an individual in pain should withdraw, find his peace however he may (even in drugs, even in death), but that withdrawal should become an evangelical movement complete with holy fervor, a movement which by definition just abandons the rest of mankind. It is so wasteful, so uncharitable. And I was struck by the pith of a question that a Negro student directed to Dr. Timothy Leary after an LSD lecture, as reported in the *Times:* "What the hell do you think is going on in this country while you cats are on those trips?"

It is amazing how fast today's parent has to run merely

to keep up with what were the dangers that loomed for his young last year. It is worse for me than for the Red Queen. I really would have been content, looking back, to remain worried about teen-age driving and all the simple, Old World perils that attach to it; how you approach your adolescent in regard to cars, sex, smoking, and drinking, and the amount of attention he pays to what you think— all of it falling into the province of youthful rebellion and what kind of rebellion your youth may be tempted by. Those subjects do occupy me and I may pick at them. But drugs have been added to this list, have moved right to the top of it and, in fact, have become a terrible thing apart. Central to the idea that there is a schismatic quality to the mores of the young today is the introduction of drugs into their folk culture. The fascination with the very idea of drugs among our local adolescents has gone so far as to put sex in second place. Unbelievable. The legal, moral, and physical aspects to drug-taking are discussed with as great partisanship as ignorance. That marijuana has unjustly been categorized as addictive, and its use punished with excessive severity is currently in our commonwealth arch-proof of the criminal hypocrisy of our society. I hold my head. And that outrage at this injustice has been elevated to the noble level of indignation directed against such social crimes as racial discrimination makes me clutch my stomach. By all means let them make the proper legal adjustments in regard to this drug. Apart from that, I believe responsible citizens only disobey the law as a consequence of profound affront to conscience. The young may not take this traditional view, but older people who encourage lawlessness for such a frivolous "right," the right to smoke marijuana, are knaves or fools, probably the latter.

Here is where I encounter one of those perils of an intellectual Pauline, Pauline the mother. I don't think it is unjust to proscribe marijuana in spite of its presumed nonaddictive quality, because I don't think that the problem is solved by correctly identifying its chemical properties. The problem concerns the tapping of attention, the sapping of energy, by tampering with the chemistry of minds and bodies, and it offends the whole of me. I would like to, but once more cannot, subscribe to that liberal permissiveness that handsomely, with largess, parades its unshockability, its absolutely endless readiness to suspend judgment. I have to draw the line.

My deep annoyance is directed against those middle-aged patrons who *understand* the young, who sob with them over the Mess We Have Made, over our hypocrisy, our Soulless Materialism, the people who are old enough to be their fathers, and in some instances *are* their fathers, and who are right there peeping at what's most outrageous, glancing back to be sure they are the farthest out, and who meanwhile lend an intellectual respectability, a moral integrity even, to a thing like taking pot. They give a bad name to liberalism, make it seem sniveling instead of tough.

Look at Aldous Huxley, they will say, for instance. Do you know that Aldous Huxley spent the last years of his life—and a deeply religious and reverent person he was—experimenting with drugs in his search for the sublime limits of human experience? Well, as I see it, and leaving aside a clinical inquiry into what led Huxley in this direction, one would say of him that by the time he was 60 he had lived an enormously involved life and contained within himself a notable corpus of emotional and intellectual data. If he, by using drugs, went delving into his own depths for "the inner kick that heightens perception, sensitivity, awareness," why at least it cannot be said that he was an empty vessel.

How can one take the same view of an 18- or 20-year-old person? Whatever is inside him is, by comparison, in a very rudimentary condition. It is surely bizarre to indulge a boy in the illusion that his own capacity for perception, his innate sensitivity, his potential awareness are immensely rich but are sleeping, and that taking drugs will wake them all up. Illusion on illusion. It smacks of the very hypocrisy and materialism over which all the sobbing is about. Take pot, the modern work-free way to heightened perception.

If you want to have your perception heightened, that is laudable. But almost everything to perceive, proportionately speaking, is outside, in the world, and if you are 20, why you have half a century of careful honing to make yourself that exquisite instrument of perception that actually does heighten your awareness and sensitivity. It's work, but you get used to it, you get to like it.

I accept that my hostile and unscientific attitude to the legalizing of marijuana derives from my being a mother, and I believe that this emotional approach is shared by most parents, and I submit that this is not irrelevant. I do not want my children to smoke marijuana. I am, furthermore, increasingly restless with the facile use of historical analogy to prove that I am reacting like kissing kin to the mountaineers of Tennessee, who so memorably and successfully defended their Bible against Scopes and science. "To the fundamentalists of Tennessee and elsewhere," says Richard Hofstadter, "the effort to stop the teaching of evolution represented an effort to save the religion of their children—indeed, to save all the family pieties." I am not without sympathy for their position.

My position is not the same. If one views American life critically and, inevitably, with moments of despair, one has these two choices: to enter it anyway and do the best one can with it, or withdraw. To me withdrawal is an unhealthy choice. It evokes my compassion but it does not cause me to equate sickness with health. I don't think sickness and health have equal rights.

We don't want our children to smoke marijuana, because we want them to confront life, not duck out of it. Let them shop around that bazaar with its psychedelic tinsel and its strange rhythmic love wail and then move along, keeping as mementos some of the bright paper flowers and the happy color, but rejecting finally the simplistic answers. We don't want them to outgrow rebellion and return to the safe embraces of conformity. On the contrary, we hope and expect that their nonconformity will be significant nonconformity and their disbelief will be *discriminating* disbelief. These are our family pieties.

Whether it is really possible or not to separate the psychiatric causes of withdrawal and of engagement from the "rational" or "philosophic" causes, I'm going to pretend it can be done. I'm going to look back at me, at our household, and by careful selection of things that fit the theory, and omission of things that belie it, describe my line of attack at being the mother of teen-agers. If it has not been successful the children can write their own books in rebuttal, and I expect they will.

To do this I must repeat what is beginning to embarrass me, that the woman is the crux of the matter, because I feel myself the crux of our success, such as it is—not the cause, but the *sine qua non*. Just as it is essentially my morale, my equilibrium, upon which the several personalities in this household float through childhood, so it is the buoyancy of the values and beliefs I transmit that are to prevent them from going under. Now I have already said that as transmitter of culture a mother cannot today be expected to act as technician, but must confine herself to the role of moral interpreter. That is what women have always been. But where I differ, and where almost all intelligent women living differ, is that we do not have a quiverful of absolutes with which to go hunting for the answers to the questions a child asks. We are all empiricists when we describe for him with warmth and sincerity what is noble, kind, good, right, but as Jean says, you'd have to be an idiot not to have reservations.

For me it is a godless, answerless world of inherent order, structure, beauty, logic, and the salient fact is the ubiquity of contradiction. Contradiction, not chaos. You live more or less successfully by making a truce with the contradictions within you and without; in fact you are forever redrawing the trucial terms, and this is what children, as they grow older, must learn to do—an especially difficult task in their teens, when they are obsessed with their search for purity, integrity, wholeness, oneness, the resolutions of all the tensions that riddle them.

The upheaval we are living through is at least throwing up new knowledge, and from this, it seems to me, we learn that we are allowed to release ourselves from an intellectual and spiritual (if not psychological) preoccupation with our personal impurity, our interior sin. It is an old habit, hard to give up, this nursing of personal sin; and it is so American. The taint of purity runs through our red, white, and blue blood, is the earliest foreign body to infect these shores. It derives from the Puritan conviction of purity, the test of saintliness, the oneness within and without through which we can merge, if chosen, with that larger Purity.

History reverberates with Catholic, Lutheran, and then (great crescendo) *Puritan* admonitions to think pure thoughts. But I do not think pure thoughts. Inside me is a really choice collection of sinful thoughts. And I cannot and never have chastised a child for his bad thoughts. For to me evil is no longer an interior but an exterior matter, a social crime, and all evil is subsumed under Cruelty, gratuitous cruelty. Beneath the wing of this evil is the old capital sin of sloth that the theologian, Harvey Cox, writes about. An English word is sloth, he tells us, and derives from the Greek words "not caring." Handy to know, since I believe that all virtue is centrifugal and spins outward from Caring.

Now if the problem is to head off a "series of psychological bangs before the one big bang," there must be constructed an ethic that first acknowledges the contradictions inside oneself and out, and then concentrates its fire on actual acts of cruelty, by commission and by omission. And second, I think this ethic must derive from the past, thereby carrying with it the widest reach of people possible, and primarily from our Judeo-Christian culture in which there is, God knows, an inexhaustible supply of symbols to cover all human behavior. To abandon that culture and start from scratch would be both elitist and naïve. And until somebody comes along and constructs the ethic, one has to do it oneself, take the heritage and pass it along with, unless you are an idiot, reservations.

Of course you can still be an idiot, reservations and all, which I will demonstrate in this sample, by describing my rapprochement with the Ten Commandments. The Ten Commandments, the little golden double tombstone, was what hung from the chain around the necks of those children in my school in the Bronx whose chains did not hold golden crosses. I never minded, one way or another, having no tablet, no cross, no chain around my own neck. I don't think I gave the Ten Commandments a thought until, some years ago when I was a quite young mother, I was struck by the injunction "Honor thy Father and Mother" and needled by the question "Suppose we aren't honorable?" This was the thin wedge, and I have since chiseled at this stone shamelessly. Three of the commandments are to me bedrock and eternal: Thou shalt not kill,

Thou shalt not steal, Thou shalt not bear false witness; and they come as close, as I see it, to being absolutes as is consonant with the human situation. I leave out adultery because it is small, not in that class, and doesn't have to be cruel or disastrous to others. The several concerning the worship of God are optional. The "coveting" interests me especially as an example of an interior problem, a sin which previous generations rode down on with a hot passion that appears now to be, at the very least, misdirected energy. Of course, if you act upon what you covet, then you may be trespassing beyond your own fantasies into a social crime, thereby breaking some other commandment.

I am very far from inviting people to agree with my assessment of these ancient and hallowed laws, but I use them as an example of how one may have to transmit the moral traditions of the past, if they are to be successfully transmitted at all. What one would want one's children to see is that there is a live relevance to their cultural heritage, but that not every part of it may be live or relevant to them. Otherwise they are liable to say goodbye to all that, tell you toodledoo, they are going off to make graven images. Somehow it seems they must accept that contradiction is elemental—and that you can covet away, for instance, but that it is the actual act of cruelty that is proscribed.

I remember loosening myself cautiously from my mother's authority, an admiring, intimidated, and obedient girl in my teens. My adolescence is a charmless blur in my memory, and I have small inclination to recall it seriously, but I do know that it was punctuated by bouts of real fury over one rule. I was expected not only to do what my mother felt must be done, regardless of my disinclination, or even disagreement, but to do whatever it was *gra-*

ciously. Graciously! Can you imagine the tax on a teen-age soul to do graciously what, upon the highest princi-ples of human autonomy, one resisted doing at all? I suffered from the soreness of this double indignity.

Now this is what an adolescent does feel, this sense of outrage that he cannot be pure and true, that he is made to perform—actually he is the most performing creature outside a circus—under adult direction. An adolescent yearns to be one single self, to be true to that self, to be all of a piece, achieve that Puritan purity. The idea of dual-ity, of inherent contradiction repels him. He wants to reconcile all the strands of strain. As would we all.

It is at this juncture that the alarmed parent may want to urge the claims of a host of discarded minor virtues lately fallen out of fashion—discretion, tact, tolerance, prudence, all those self-reining erstwhile goodnesses that hedge the contradictory quality of life, screen it, contain it. When you try, it may seem like talking through a glass wall.

But to be mature is to bring good grace to what your mind, having registered its reservations, sees must be done. It is a sullied condition, compromising, impure, trucial. And I find that in spite of my having bridled so painfully at my mother's expectations—and I wince when I say this—I have approached my own children somewhat along the same lines. We are a big family, I say, and we are all dependent to some extent on a certain minimum pulling together lest we undermine each other. We need, and you are expected to come through with proper spirit, especially in times of stress. Think your own thoughts but, you know, good show. I don't want to squelch those true selves, only to civilize them.

That the healthy, mature, civilized thing to do is to accept the irreconcilability of things and not cry about it, is my bias. The adolescent may resist, but the mature woman sees the thing intuitively. The immature woman, being still all out for self-realization, meaning by that something pure and unpolluted and nonexistent, she may tend to foul her nest.

CHAPTER 11

On the Guilt of Parents

I do not behave like a man who has lost his dignity; but I also know that people who do not lose their dignity in the presence of certain things have none to lose.

THOMAS MANN

Stunned by the force of my own argument, I may, in my exaltation, have seemed to describe the winning of a battle of parenthood, whereas I was only meaning it to be the rough sketch of a skirmish. It is very appealing, this idea that one can, by a process of judicious selection, transmit a critical but humane appraisal of life to members of the next generation, without tipping them over into revulsion, or shocking them into numbness, or causing their retreat into self-absorption. It should work, but it often doesn't. Furthermore, in line with my habit of giving with the right hand and taking with the left, I have laid an excessive onus on the mother, and now I want to say that it is not hers exclusively, I know. But mine is a personal, nonacademic essay into these human relations, and I do not want to seem to lend my husband's professional authority to what I say. In our particular case, we are nearly always, father and mother, staunchly united against the assaults of our young; and with our last breath, which may be any day now, we will affirm that we are not vanquished by them.

The other impression I must correct, or even reverse, is the portrait of myself as mother who, while alas lacking the inner glow of pure thoughts, charges through this house with rational ones. When I was much younger, my pretensions more modest, and I suffered an attack of self-examination, I would admit to myself, with a giggle of shock, that my dreams and aspirations fleshed themselves out, so to speak, through the ignoble and trivial but unmistakable influence of the Hollywood of my youth. "Whence, Mrs. Seton," should somebody ever ask me the question, "did your interest in journalism spring?" "Whence?" would I have to say "From Cary Grant and Rosalind Russell at the Saturday matinees." It wasn't so much becoming a writer, or looking like Rosalind Russell that captured my interest, but merely being the preoccupation of Cary Grant. All this still holds.

It holds for me and it holds for an awful lot of people who are old enough to have spent our childhood Saturday afternoons watching the double feature at the local cinema, and it is not simply a giggling matter. We have not come out into the daylight of our lives altogether unseared by the simple moral message, repeated from Mickey Rooney to Bing Crosby, in westerns, in easterns, from poverty to riches: Virtue Is Rewarded.

"If you had loved that child. . . . If you had taken proper care of him. . . ."

"If you were not off to play bridge every afternoon, but there when she came home from school. So that she could turn to you, talk to you. . . ."

It is the august, black-robed judge, looking like Lewis

Stone out of Andy Hardy, who leans across his dais to scold the Really Guilty Ones, the parents of children in trouble with the law. This is not only pop morality, this is what the judge really says, what we all to some extent really believe. As you sow so shall you reap, says the judge.

But unlawful behavior is merely the reflection of one branch of parental failure. Suppose, Judge Hardy, you're always home in the afternoons, but she won't talk to you, and you have been worried to death by her sullenness and her silence, or her loneliness and her pain? What if you did love that child and took great care of him and he is resentful, hostile, detached? This is the reality that Hollywood smothered. It is part of the American creed that punishment in these United States always fits the crime, that around here there is a great and divine and frightening (and simple) justice, you can count on it.

But the evidence to the contrary has been accumulating with formidable force these past few years, and it is one of those instances where you may really become quite bowed down with reservations. I know parents who ache with worry and guilt; and the guilt is distributed, in a vague way, over misdeeds in the handling of their children that are too petty, too undistinguished, too guileless to produce a consequence of so much misery, misery for the child and for his hovering, balked, uncertain parents.

These are children who had their head start from the moment they opened their eyes. Society has never thought to rescue them, gather them up when they were 3 years old, and teach them how to live, to read, to play, to hope, to reach for the future, because in their own tiny life span there was too little caring, not enough to eat, no father, an inarticulate, overburdened mother. It is sometimes said that for children of the slum the worst deprivation is the lack of language. They don't have the words with which to explore their thoughts and feelings. That is what stunts their lives, why they need to be sought out when they are still practically babies. That is what Head Start aims for.

But our children this side of the poverty belt run the gamut of blessings. They bear, no doubt, the middle class mark of having been overfed, overdressed, over-stimulated by discussions and explanations, and in a world of talk, talk, talk, they have hardly missed the sweet uses of vocabulary. I once read in the *Times* that the average American talks eleven minutes a day. Imagine the vast reservoir of silent people necessary to balance households like ours, where we've all used up our allotted time by breakfast.

I'm talking about children who are articulate, which is to say that they can explore themselves, communicate with others (though some can't or won't), who are loved and cared for, and who should be buoyant and healthy and land on their feet. But sometimes, anyhow, a child like that is crushed or disabled, and he plots his own course for failure right through that benign environment, unswayed by parents and teachers who are desperate to help him.

Now I don't mean to say that these young are outside the laws of cause and effect, that the mothers are pure and the fathers are guiltless. But so often the parents are people whose behavior has been neither criminal nor debauched, who have produced only the pedestrian run of mistakes and tensions, who are probably most guilty of fumbling, and who are at worst awkward in their attempts to make amends. Fumbling, being awkward, are unsuccesses that contain their own apologies, pleas for mercy. How could mankind have survived until today if that sort of human frailty costs so much, is so destructive?

All Hollywood chapter and verse came to that simple

consensus message: Virtue Is Rewarded. It skimmed off the creamy, easy religious homilies and gave us Bing Crosby Christianity. The happy ending presupposed a very simple Divine Apparatus that told right from wrong so well that your 9-year-old self could agree a hundred per cent. I have the feeling that for my generation the Sunday morning service was preached down by that Saturday matinee. Of course, before Hollywood, there was a Christianity with a just God whose ways were mysterious, who, in His infinite wisdom, let man be grief-ridden, tempted, seduced, let him fall. The reward for virtue was not on this earth.

My generation were children when the gas ovens of Germany were being constructed, adolescents by the time Hiroshima was bombed, but we did not absorb their meaning, as nobody yet can, and arrived at the other end of World War II ready for marriage and children. We have been the parents who meant to be compassionate, understanding and rational people, instructed by the newest psychological insights. Be loving, open, honest, earnest, and you have an airtight system for child-rearing. Your children could not help but flourish with things so wholesome. It is virtue being rewarded, scientifically based.

There has been no room in these child-rearing theories of the postwar decades for an inscrutable God, and for man as an essentially tragic figure. Now I have been remembering Milton's *Paradise Lost* that I studied a long time ago, because of the argument that has revolved around it since it was written. Milton, it is said, made Satan too magnificent, too powerful and attractive, a too unequal match for man. "High on a throne of royal state . . . Satan exalted sat, by merit rais'd to that bad eminence"—the merit of being an adversary worthy of the enormous and yet more magnificent God the Father. It is a conflict of wills between the might of good and the might of evil, and the pawns were little clay creatures with life breathed into them, with a Divine spark, only a spark. Nothing next to Satan exalted, as it turns out.

Milton left man too frail to cope with this bad eminence, and ever since, theologians have been nervous about *Paradise Lost;* for it follows that if man is no match for Satan, God has been Imperfect and Unjust in his arrangement of the universe.

As can be seen, I don't leave theology alone, and I am as much struck by my temerity as the next fellow. I am fascinated in this instance by the symbolic conjecture that God simply didn't give man the breadth he needed, if not to keep the devil at bay, at least to recognize and anticipate the difficulties in being honorably human. A spark is too little. I suppose a modern theologian would say that you are playing God yourself if you believe that your compassion and reason and your *will* as parents will determine the successful character and health of your children.

As it is, we are living with an amalgam of the Hollywood and the Milton views. Lots of our children are coming along sturdily because we have made good parents and virtue is being rewarded; and some of our children are not, for reasons that are mysterious, inscrutable; and we are helpless in our despair. Parents will watch, sometimes in anger, sometimes in anguish, their girl or boy of 16, 18, 20 *not* take hold of life, *not* feel its joy and challenge, in spite of what ought to have been a promising childhood and what should be a promising future. Though even as they lived with that child through that promising childhood they sensed some lack of connection.

There is no question that there are always psychiatric explanations for these crippling emotional patterns, and if this or that young person is lucky, psychiatric help. What is bedeviling is why one girl should be so selfish and close-minded, brought up as she has been, in a generous and open-minded family; why another will be debilitated by awful depressions when she has been loved and admired from her infancy; why a bright boy didn't learn to read well, muddled through his schooling, is dropping out of everything; why another drifts into drug-taking, drag-racing, anything numbing and superficial. Why do such large things happen from such petty causes? Why such terrible punishments for such little crimes?

Again it was Hollywood theology that kept Practically Everybody in good shape, that created the image of the thriving Average American with his house and his car and his fair-haired children, that filled the world with Ordinary People coping very well with life in a plain, commonsensical way. It probably wasn't Hollywood who thought it all up, but it was Hollywood that spread it so thick. This myth, the belief in every man's successful pursuit of happiness, is our political doctrine, too. It is the democratization of the good life, the giving to every American what in the old world had been reserved for the chosen few.

But outside this egalitarian dream world of success and happiness for all in the history and literature of the West, there is no such acceptance that virtue and its rewards are the normal state of things. From our Old Testament roots, from ancient Greece, comes man, the tragic figure, the wanderer in the wilderness: Oedipus didn't *know* it was his mother he had married. "Honor thy Father and Mother" was an *order*, not an expectation. Nobody thought Lear *deserved* his two cruel daughters, nor le Père Goriot his. The great characters of fiction don't tell us how to master life, but how poignant and complex it is; and the themes of the generations, *Fathers and Sons, Sons and Lovers*, weave through the very greatest fiction as well as through the oldest fairy tales. "There was a miller

127

and he had three sons . . ." and two were bad. "Once upon a time there was an old woman who had three daughters . . ." but only one was good. Ordinary People have a lot of trouble, the Average Man is a poor fool, misery begets misery. To land on your feet is a rare trick.

If one looks at one's own hearth from this perspective, the father does not have to be drunk, the mother always out playing bridge—parents, that is, do not have to be guilty of gross misbehavior in order to merit an unhappy child. If they have mismanaged, it is not necessarily because they are bad or stupid but because human nature is enormously intricate; the growth of character, the interaction between personalities infinitely varied, complex, and unpredictable. We don't need these scoldings from Judge Hardy. We bear the guilt willy-nilly. But perhaps we are making things harder for ourselves by forgetting the more profound assessment of the nature of man that predates Hollywood and survives Hollywood, the tragic view of man, for whom a spark has not been enough.

CHAPTER 12

On Grown Girls and Sexual Freedom

Civilization always needs to wrap up the idea of love in veils of fancy, to exalt and refine it, and thereby to forget cruel reality. The solemn or graceful game of the faithful knight or the amorous shepherd, the fine imagery of courtly allegories, however brutally life belied them, never lost their charm nor all their moral value. The human mind needs these forms, and they always remain essentially the same.

HUIZINGA

Although I now believe in teenagers and I still have no religion, each of our children has elected at 8 or 9 to make an independent choice and join some friend on Sunday mornings to become part of a religious communion for a year or so. Thus Jenny went off to the First Church Congregational with Sarah Cohen—this is a very ecumenical town—to sing in the choir. One Family Sunday when I

129

was there to hear her, the minister took for his sermon "The Wise and the Foolish Virgins," and as my mind slipped sideways from his text I thought, virgins, wise and foolish, are a vanishing breed, along with the manservants and the maidservants. And here I am, the mother of so many girls, knowing I would be foolish to teach them simply that the sum and substance of "morality" is the overriding obligation to arrive at the altar in that condition of purity which has been traditionally esteemed, and wondering what would be wise. It would be foolish to discount the aura of sexual freedom already well established on the campus even if all that insouciance, that beautiful self-confidence, long hair and thighs, were only the moment's mask, while underneath, the statistics about virginity, etc., as the sociologists tell us, have been the same for decades. I only half believe in sociologists, and I don't believe at all in these statistics.

I was on a Fifth Avenue bus in New York a couple of years ago, happily and openly examining the girl standing nearby for twenty blocks. This is what people from out-of-town feel they can do in New York: stare, as though looking at natives was what one puts one's nickels in the slot for. She was about 20, this girl, with white lacy stockings clasped daintily at the instep of her foot by the patent leather straps of enormous Mary Janes, size 10. Five feet eight inches up a black velvet ribbon held back her long, long hair. She wore a demure Chesterfield coat with black velvet collar and the total effect, carefully calculated, triumphantly achieved, was that of a huge little girl, Alice after she had eaten the cake. This Alice was giggling about the sight she was and regularly nuzzled the shoulder of her escort for cover.

The escort by her side was nobody, a bean. He really needed a beard, long hair, something to put him into the show. And as I watched them I found I had a sympathetic feeling for a 20-year-old girl who wants to look as though she'd been brought by Gulliver from a nursery in Brobdingnag. In 1946 when I was 20—something I mention to give historical perspective, though it pains me—the great thing was to appear mature, experienced, even world-weary. Black was not for velvet ribbons but for Advanced Views, a suggestion that you had your own apartment, dated older men—at least until school reopened. The very last thing would have been to look innocent, to dress as though you didn't know what you were doing.

Now to dress as though you didn't know what you were doing was, I think, the very aim and goal of this Alice on the bus. Her clothes were protective coloration. Today's girl of 20 has moved into a society of such unprecedented freedom that probably the only one to believe there is a Code of Behavior to protect her is her mother. Her mother who lives in Pittsfield, Massachusetts, or Chattanooga, Tennessee.

The very word "protection," once foursquare, is now square. If the boys are looking curly and girlish, neither like cavemen nor knights in armor nor cowboys, drugstore or ranch-type, it is because the muscley man useful for Defending Virtue and Rescuing Virgins has become redundant. And to look as though you are a Ravager of Maidens is a quite unnecessary demonstration of strength.

Change is so quick today, adjustment so rapid, and there may be no more accurate test of pace than to mark the flashes of shock to our sense of propriety that the young send through us. Indeed I believe we are shock-happy and can no longer marshal up indignation, to say nothing of effective opposition. We watch the "little girl" look give way to the gay, sweet, open-eyed, innocent trollop, and what will come next is beyond guessing. This year our Julie, who only last week emerged from babyhood, walks off into her world in the miniest skirts permitted under arbitrary paternalistic rule, turtlenecked at the top, sheathed in the high slim London boots she spent her dowry on, the only stretch of her exposed being an alarming expanse of thigh. Grudgingly I admire the effect of her costume, her cheerful gait, and I think what is missing in the picture is a whip. It is strange to be reminded of the Marquis de Sade since she is as ingenuous as Alice, and all the hippiest of adornments are meant to be the paraphernalia of joyful innocence. The young have been fooling with the Cult of Innocence for some time, and this is merely the current guise of free-loving and uncorrupted Children of Nature. Nothing human that is pleasurable, peaceable, and superficial is alien to them.

Whatever is the costume, it is still recognizable as part of the dance of life, the "wrapping of the idea of love in veils of fancy" through which boy and girl ultimately want to find each other, want to become man and woman. I believe the human mind needs these forms, but I wonder whether Huizinga would find, in beat and hip, forms of courtship that are essentially the same as those of earlier epochs? Perhaps the thread of sameness is this presumption of innocence, although in our time this innocence is so shrill, so flamboyant, so often vulgar that it is taken for its opposite.

There is in me this conservative core that is always looking for rocks to stand on in the shifting sands. I need to find fixed and immutable aspects to the relationship of man and woman, and so I find them. I find them by refusing to accept a viable alternative to a stable family for the rearing of offspring. No state nurseries, no amount of educational toys and psychological insight and high protein diet are acceptable substitutes for a mother and a father. Something of the traditional reverence for family life must be rescued, made relevant, and passed on. How is one to make inroads into today's presumptuous innocence, a bold, open-ended innocence, indifferent to all cultural strictures? That's what one asks oneself.

We are still linked, although tenuously, with the guilt and innocence of the past. The pivotal social disaster has always been the conceiving of a child out of wedlock, and it continues to contain the elements of disaster. Until our abortion laws are substantially liberalized, or a pill is marketed that will perform as an afterthought, the problem of an unwanted child will stay with us. If, today, a young girl finds herself pregnant, and her father does not throw her out of doors into a snow storm, why that is certainly an advance. If he does not press her into an unsuitable marriage, that is progress too. But the alternatives that remain are still painful and destructive for herself and her baby, from abortion and its shady and sordid atmosphere, through the putting of one's own child up for adoption, with all the wrenching misery that it entails, to the keeping of the child, whose life can hardly escape a kind of Biblical taint.

I have heard from several sources that it is not unusual for an unmarried student, in reply to the question of a sympathetic doctor or social worker, "Why, at least, didn't you use some form of contraceptive?" to answer, "Oh, I couldn't. It would be so calculating!" It now seems to me that there is no longer room for this much innocence and ingenuousness. A girl who can say that, is not a *bad* girl, quite obviously, but tender and sensitive and cruelly immature, a once foolish virgin.

I would like our girls to remain tender and sensitive, but I believe that long before they are eighteen they ought to understand thoroughly that pregnancies out of wedlock and illegitimacy are not leftover taboos from some former and outmoded morality but are perpetual taboos which protect the sanity of humankind. Whatever romantic dreams and attachments they may have in their lives should never escape the calculation of this taboo at least.

To talk over this much with one's growing girls is not so hard, but to cover the issue of birth control is to move into an area that I believe is infinitely more delicate. For it is not, I think, seemly for a mother to be too explicit, to intrude too intimately into this aspect of an older daughter's life, because it seems like a mother's endorsement or complicity in a relationship which by definition ought to be private to her child. In fact, what one often considers on the question of what or what not to teach one's young is whether, by the very discussion of such an issue as premarital relations or contraception, you, as the mother, are lending a touch of acceptability to what might otherwise remain unthinkable. But where in today's America would it remain unthinkable?

If the world's great crisis is overpopulation, if, as it is said, we are in greater danger from sexual than from atomic energy, it is no wonder that sexual implications attach themselves to every tentative solution to every economic, political, and social problem that exists. Our children, in the fifth, sixth, and eighth grades study South America and each country in it three times over—possibly a case of overcompensation for the neglect of our day, when we learned only that the Amazon was its largest river and then went on to Australia. Ask Maggie what is the insurmountable obstacle to progress in South America and she will answer "overpopulation" without hesitating. "But," a twelve-year-old is likely to ask, "why do people have children that they don't want?" And to a child of that age one can talk impersonally about the force of physical passion in grown-up people, about birth control and the moral considerations and religious doubts that the Catholic Church has kept alive in our minds.

It is the reverence for life and the mystery of birth that

are what the Church honors and what one would somehow want to convey in all its solemnity to one's young. It
is the awe one may feel before an old Italian painting of
the Visitation, where the Virgin Mary and Saint Elizabeth
gravely bend toward each other to touch their cheeks in
recognition that each is carrying a holy child. I have felt
solemn and reverent toward life when carrying a child. I
could no more have felt this with a child I didn't want
than a child I couldn't feed.

Once when Maggie was about ten and drawing up her
life plans—chemistry, psychiatry, and the clarinet—I
asked her whether she wasn't going to be a mother too.
"Oh, I want to be a mother," she said, with reassuring
ardor, "but I don't see how I'm going to have the time."
Time she will have, although she may be 57 years old
when she's finished with her training. The girls are lucky
to be living now not only because, in the language of
sociologists, they will have so many "options" in the way
of life work, but because, in the language of love, they
will be released from the pressures of early marriage,
hasty marriage, and the wrong marriage, and from the
distress of unwanted pregnancies.

Even so, I regard the sexual freedom of the campus
with mixed feelings, very mixed. When I told one of my
friends that I was brooding about what sort of moral
teaching was likely to be useful for today's adolescent
girls, she said, "Moral teaching! Good heavens, Cynthia,
that cake is all eaten up!" It amuses her to catch me again
earnestly trying to pat together crumbling pieces of the
past and present, to salvage some traditional point of
behavior or code of honor, some private idol from the
clean sweep of the iconoclasts.

But I have another friend who is probably far more
representative of American parents, and who is not only
horrified by the sexual permissiveness among late ado-

lescents and young adults but, like a general in the army, drilled her daughter, who was about to enter a school of nursing, to withstand five years under siege. Five years at the edge of a pit is what it was, and on no account was Betty to fall into it. "Five years until she gets her degree is too long," said the mama. "She'll never make it. She'll have to get married." "But there are so many possibilities open to her that were never open to us," I said, "and isn't the highest goal a good marriage?" "Two things I don't swallow," she bellowed, "are Free Love and God is Dead!"

Free Love! My heavens, it sounds like what the Twenties were roaring about. It echoes with a wholesome, nostalgic, high principled cry that makes you want to rally to the banner of D. H. Lawrence. What we call the Sexual Revolution is something else, not dreamlike at all, and a *fait accompli*. It is on beyond principle. Sexual freedom and equality already exist on the campus no matter how stoutly mama may object to it, and entail such a swift shift of mores that it is little wonder there is a parental lag in recognizing and coping with them. I believe this sexual revolution is irreversible and that nothing will restore the ancient concepts of innocence short of a political revolution of the extreme right or left that could revive and enforce some sort of cult of purity. Better, as always, to come to terms with freedom.

This doesn't necessarily mean that large numbers of our college girls are tumbling, but only that any one among them who does is not in danger of encountering ostracism from her peers, or even providing a sensation for her friends. Young girls, smart or dumb, gifted or drifty, tend to have a part of themselves wanting to be in love and searching and wondering and feeling tender about now one and now another young man, and today, this may go on for years and years under the kindly auspices of their open-minded, nonjudgmental contemporaries.

The question for parents is how to prepare one's daughters for this freedom, how have them profit from its latitude and from the time it so generously provides for the making of decisions? And how, meanwhile, to see that they find their sea legs, don't get sick and tumble overboard—that they preserve their self-esteem, their personal standards? The answer will depend upon what you mean by standards. If all you mean to convey is what Eliza Doolittle meant to convey by repeating at intervals, "I'm a good girl, I am," then it is a narrow technical point, and I don't know how a mother can successfully insist upon it.

But it is worth noting Eliza Doolittle, with her inherent nobility, held her head high, did not prize herself lightly. And here, I think, comes the crux of all one would want one's daughter to learn to be. To be somebody whose sense of human worth and dignity, while embracing all mankind, includes herself.

And as it seems as likely as ever that she will want to marry and have children, she will have to prepare herself, mind and heart, in the midst of this unprecedented and beckoning freedom, to settle down in the end with one man, to stand more or less faithfully by the family they plant for possibly fifty years as the actuarial charts have it. And does a girl pick up the habit of fidelity by skipping lightly from love to love before coming upon one that seems durable? And, on the other hand, can one expect, statistically speaking, that for everybody the right man is going to be the first man that a girl loves? To be excused from a mistaken choice is surely a good thing.

Now I don't think that for our daughters the years between their leaving our house and the establishing of their own are a Yawning Gulf. Not at all. I think of them as an elm-shaded, ivy-creeping pause, a pause in which they may thrive and flourish in glorious freedom, a freedom that is benign and not perilous, provided they escape the perils.

The perils are peculiar to the age. By all odds the worst

aspect of this campus freedom is the way it invades the last corners of privacy, the way it pursues the silent, the shy, the reserved, the frightened. Everybody is rooted out. There are no sanctuaries. At our neighboring Smith College, the girls have finally gained permission to have boys visit their rooms at fixed hours during the weekend, and I agree that it is entirely reasonable to want to be alone, the boy and the girl together, even if only to talk politics. More than that, I believe it is a necessity when two people long to withdraw by themselves, that some place be available. But the even greater need for privacy belongs to the girl who has only her dormitory room to slip into, an upstairs room that has been free, up to now, of group pressures, joyous noises, all the sights and sounds of the chase. I remember with what relief I ducked into my own college room to escape exposure when I was feeling raw-nerved and not wanting to be tracked down and found out.

This leads to a fact that I find reprehensible to dismiss: that women, in love relationships, react more slowly and more deeply than do men. They need to shield themselves from the too superficial and too frequent and too callous encounters that men, evidently, are able to take lightly. They like to pretend, today's young, that the great liberation of women from the duplicity and hypocrisy of the double standard allows a girl the same light pleasures and (with the pill and all) the same freedom from responsibility and consequence that the men have always had. But I don't believe this is true. A woman's nature is not a man's, and it is not easy or natural for her to become casually promiscuous without distorting her capacity for an eventual permanent relationship. She isn't naturally a sower of wild oats. She isn't a sower. A man, or as we have it from history and literature, some men, fly through their youths enjoying girl after girl, as forgetful as drones, and after a while put the past behind them and settle down. A young woman, however, is not really like White's queen bee, because while she may find herself attracted now to one man and now to another, she can't *flit* between them. She is not forgetful. More of herself is engaged in making love, more time is necessary for her to disengage herself.

Up to now, in any case, there has been this physiological or emotional rhythmic complicity contributing to the success of the grand reproductive design, a rhythm that inclines a woman toward a permanent relationship. The question is whether all the strength that nature has heretofore exerted to keep the race moving along will be adequate to meet what is surely the unlooked for, unpredictable counterforce produced by electronic engineering. Modern systems of communication have produced yet another kind of revolution. Through television and the movies they bring to front stage center the most sensational of contemporary unorthodox behavior, behavior that one would have had to seek before this age of exposure far out, at the fringe. And by this focus they remove the qualities that kept this behavior remote, bizarre, and unattractive to all but those special few with special needs. And they invest this behavior with star qualities, with familiarity, make it the exciting motif of life today, and say to the young: you too can be beat, can be hip, can turn on, can love-in. I've accused the drug takers of being evangelical, but who would they reach without the media? Could sexual attitudes flipflop so fast without the flood of cinema and TV films and books to show us how?

I don't compare the two hazards, drugs and sexual freedom, and in fact must repeat that I believe women coming of age today are very lucky. But freedom and excess are in yoke, as usual. In an experimental way one can slide into promiscuity, and promiscuity is drugging to the female sensibilities, depending as it does upon skimming quickly by relationships, glancing off them, thereby imperceptibly numbing a woman's capacity to go deep. Any form of drugging is frightening to me.

It's no use to prepare our girls to defend their "innocence" when "innocence" is the hallmark of the young, what they have discovered and what they are celebrating. It is their "thing," and we would not be talking the same language. I want to prepare them to withstand not seduction by men but seduction by simple ideas, simple answers. The perils are excess, social intimidation, promiscuity, ingenuousness. I want to nail it all down, and it takes a long time, years.

One is not finished with the matter of sex once having delivered that initial awkward description of procreation to a 10-year-old daughter. It is the mere laying of the foundations. For in the course of the next three or four years, before adolescence has intruded and robbed you entirely of this once familiar and lovable girl child, you will have to use your time well to establish a base of understanding in what is still a matter-of-fact, impersonal, reasonable, and unimpassioned little head. After she has learned the facts of life, but while she still finds them silly and disassociates herself forever from such unbelievable behavior, she must hear you put flesh and heart and mind to those facts. She ought to know thoroughly that bearing a child is just the very beginning of the obligations its family has to it. She has to see first how deeply rooted has been the respect for chastity in women, and why. Let that settle in and then after a while she must hear from you, from her mother, that the prohibitions underpinning chastity are being removed by methods of birth control. There are no more scarlet letters, no more bastard children to bring disgrace, few social stigmas to scare one into restraint. The young man's expectation that his wife will have known no other man may linger with older people. But there has been a quick last spin of the sexual revolution and in a trice the expectation has disappeared from the minds of the young. Through the years during which you explore together the site of that line between the blessings and drawbacks of this sexual freedom, it should become clear to her, in an academic way, that love and passion and impulsive behavior are among the oldest facts of life, and that the pill is among the newest.

I think a brief can be made, if not for chastity, for circumspection. The disappearance of wise and foolish virgins is not unrelated to the supply of wise and foolish mothers. Or perhaps it is a foolish corner we are painted into. It's as if when virginity ceased to be the single crucial guarantee of goodness we were bereft of anything to say. We had to abandon the entire code of social conditioning that had depended on it, that nice parcel of minor virtues—delicacy, personal pride, grace, charm, tenderness, restraint—with all the rearing and guiding and nurturing necessary to it, because by the removal of virginity as the proof of morality, "virtue" lost its scientific basis.

CHAPTER 13

The Permissive Society

To know is nothing at all; to imagine is everything.
ANATOLE FRANCE

One of our daughters who now wishes anonymity, having heretofore reveled in notoriety from the time she could make out her name in newsprint, a daughter who is a divine and admirable and most satisfactory teen-ager, who rarely sends me through this house bellowing, "I'm not going to make it! I'm not going to make it!" more than once a day—this daughter, on the matter of The Permissive Society, is my handy foil.

Now when I was this child's age, or perhaps a couple of years older, and was first exposed to a version of Freud furnished by my contemporaries, I marveled that a man of such scholarly renown could find life so sexually permeated, that a sober intellectual of Victorian refinement could discover sexual ramifications running through our ordinary everyday lives. Whatever could he have been thinking? Well . . .

Our girls are coming of age when the entertainment

world and those in the culture trade with joy and artistry, and tastelessness and cynicism are making explicit all that has been implicit in the procreative act. And lots more. "Anything Goes" was the title of *Newsweek's* survey of the sexual scene in America, and when the daughter above-mentioned had read it, she said to me, "Well, what do you think?"

"They're going to spoil everything."

So many public spirited people are making how-to movies and writing how-to books and taking the clothes off all the lady stars—but you can only take so many clothes off, and there you are left with nothing to wonder about. Fresh in my mind was the film *Reflections in a Golden Eye* in which Elizabeth Taylor walks upstairs naked and looking much like a 40-year-old woman given to overeating (and I know whereof I speak) might be expected to appear from the rear. I find this reassuring. I mean, you know, the gods having clay feet sort of thing, although in this instance, not clay and not feet (And in fact it was not her rear but her stand-in's, as somebody told me later. Make of that what you will.) I watched this realistic cinematic treatment of a southern lady making her way to the second floor on a hot night, and I kept my cool.

"You have to get to the point where people aren't shocked any more," explains someone helping them to get there. I was not shocked by *Reflections*, and I am not shocked by scenes of naked lovemaking but I sometimes squirm uneasily, feeling I am being made to peek at somebody else's most private relationship. I am not a voyeur by nature, and I don't believe, *really*, that the national interest will benefit by my learning to be one. Instead of being liberated, I feel I am being shamed, that my own privacy isn't respected but mocked. It is like having us all join together in the dark to be exposed, and it arouses in me the distress that no private, intimate relationship may belong to myself alone but must be flung broadcast across a super-sized screen.

A publisher devoted to the public weal explains, "We are working toward the last gasp. We will publish a book that will make the public gasp for the last time. When we do, we will have reached a more adult civilization." Good grief, they are going to spoil everything.

Meanwhile, though the rest of America has been having this honest and healthy confrontation with sexuality (with other people's sexuality), I have been going on with the housework, and by curious coincidence, keeping myself amused with Ella Fitzgerald singing the songs of my youth. Did you know Cole Porter wrote "Anything Goes" in 1934, when I was seven years old?

Our questioning Daughter X is so devoted to the music of her own generation that her record player is never turned off, even when she is listening to mine. And when she heard Ella singing, *I get no kick from cocaine./ I'm sure that if/ I took even one sniff/ that would bore me terrif/ ically too./ Cause I get a kick out of you,* she exclaimed, "Cocaine, Mother! They had cocaine in those days?" I murmur assent.

"You know what is awfully nice about those old songs is that you can sing them. You can hear the words and you can sing them," she said wistfully.

"Oh, that is right!" I burst, awash in nostalgia. "You can sing songs and you can be in love with love, which is such an enormously exhilarating, time-consuming thing that cocaine, let alone LSD and pot, is simply a bore by comparison."

And then, inspired by love for love, and love for her, and love for a younger me, I told it to her, told it the way it really was. In matters of the heart you can't go straight to the heart of the matter. That's the way to spoil everything. What is this thing called love? Nothing explicit. It's singing songs, painting the town, only two for tea, dear. Nothing explicit, it's all suggestive. And it takes *time*, time, postponement, self-control, and the tension builds and romance is wrapped in a tissue of colored fancy and you wait, and you sing and agonize, and wait some more and wonder whether it is love. It is romance. Romance is a great welling time-taking preliminary.

"It's just one of those things, X, dear," I said.

Now I've put it that way, I wonder whether the real structural fallacy of the permissive child-rearing theory, besides its having no structure, is this slaughtering of time. I do not like to miss an opportunity to take a furious poke at this theory, and I've followed the arguments of two or three other people who have tied the cause, Permissive Child Rearing, to the effect, our Permissive Society. Some of the strands, I agree, run straight through; the supreme importance of the present moment—whatever the present moment is—and its corollary, the immediate gratification of present desires—whatever present desires might be. But as with everything else, the reasons why we are where we are must be nearly infinite.

Hippie philosophy was permissivism's finest, brightest artificial flower. It petrified the present. We may like to blame the hippies for all the sexual acting out, but they have been only a consequence and a parody, and as they pass from the scene, melting into round pools of ghee like Little Black Sambo's tigers, they will not take the problem away with them.

I don't see how you can manage life without turning the passage of time to your use, sending latticework up through it, and then pulling yourself along. A child, before this last generation or so, was brought up almost exclusively with an eye to his future prospects. To this end went his training, secular and religious; to this end was directed the family effort and whatever could be spared in the way of funds. He must always have looked at himself as in progress through the passage of time. And since the end product was of such singular consequence, his august and remote parents probably eyed him as something in a very raw state with much work yet to be done. Thus preoccupied with distant results, people didn't give much attention to gratifying little wishes.

Permissivism was a severe reaction. The child was no longer raw stuff to be disciplined and hewn and polished to end as a man. He arrived complete. In a sense you might see it that what was eliminated was the purpose for his existence. He was not in a perpetual state of becoming. He was the end. Eliminate a serious higher purpose to a child's existence and, besides tampering with the evolution of his sense of consequence, of worth, you have left him unhitched to the significance of time: time passing, time to come, taking time, waiting, preparing, learning discipline, restraint, control to some future end, some purpose at a distance in time. Reaching puberty in this condition, with nobody to consider more important than himself, and with a crop of new talents and faculties and desires sprouting and seeming urgent, and accustomed as he has been to instant gratification, it is not unreasonable that he turn an impatient ear to adult wisdom which now, all of a sudden, says Wait! Wait? Why wait? How wait? Wait for what?

The justification for the defrocking of our sexual mores so that we can all gasp our last gasp is that it will bring us to a final acceptance of sex as a simple animal appetite. I don't share that opinion. It may be a simple appetite for animals but not for humans. I believe that in regard to people, that part of you is as personal and complicated and contradictory as the rest of yourself is. And furthermore I think that in the person who grows, whose mind becomes more finely honed, whose aesthetic taste develops, that his capacity to love, in all the ways mankind can love, broadens correspondingly. To insist that, basically, man's sexuality is as forthright as that of the lower primates is to ground it, to bring it way down to what it must be for numb and truncated people today, and to what it must historically have been for the numb and truncated masses all the way back into the past. Why would you want to do that?

It is manners, grace, convention, art and literature—it is civilization—that can let one touch the sublime. I am for civilization and this civilizing process.

Ah-ha! It may well be countered, this so-called civilizing process has repressed our natures by its fearful, salacious, taboo-ridden approach to sexuality. It has so warped and thwarted us that we are an immature anxiety-driven society. Ah-ha, yes, and ah-ha, no. You have to be selective, you have to discriminate.

Oh how divine sex is, how madly passionate we all can be, is, I take it, the message, and also more evidence of our craving for simple answers. Bring down the barriers, exorcise the taboos without pity, liberate the natural man, bare the whole truth, and spoil everything. There is a conviction among the military that you can bomb a people until they fall on their knees and cry for mercy—and you bomb them and bomb them and they don't fall on their knees and everything is broken and shattered and destroyed except the conviction in the minds of the military. And there is this parallel conviction in the minds of some thinking people that you can bludgeon the hypocrisy out of us by scatology, by mocking our sexual mores out of existence. When we all make love with joy, like the birds and the bees, we will be released from tension and free to become peaceful, integrated, and unpolluted.

Our Jenny has been studying the bees for a school

project, and she told me very soberly that the reason the bee dies when he stings his enemy is that there are barbs on his stinger, and when he tries to withdraw his stinger the barbs hold fast in the body of his enemy, and what he pulls out are his own vital organs. In my mind the voice of this 10-year-old girl is lovely for the way she says "vital organs." Her tongue cannot thoroughly manage "l's" but her mind can thoroughly manage the sad irony in the bee's situation.

The conviction that total sexual freedom, cleared of all romance, all restraint, is the answer to alienation and aggression and all the bad things, is a conviction that isn't budged by evidence of the sense of debasement, the absence of satisfaction, the accentuation of loneliness that is the experience of so many of the liberated young girls who mate casually with a series of liberated young boys. The vital organs in man are not merely biological.

And the conviction that by shocking people with explicit naked sexual acts in words or on the screen you make them more frank and less fearful—this part of the conviction isn't shaken either by the evidence that this exposure can also make people numb and indifferent, and insensitive to the subtlety of the intimate play between a man and a woman. It is true that these scenes have been treated with great artistry, but it is truer that much more often they are vulgar, and they coarsen.

A more adult civilization, will it be? Maybe. In the meantime we are now being demoralized, an apt word. And at bottom we are demoralized, I believe, because we are suffering a deprivation of fancy, of romance, of moral certitude, a sense of personal worth, and therefore we cannot throw our lines into the future. We are wrung out. And the telling evidence of this deprivation is the way so many chosen children seem to be suffering. They are not charging boldly, wickedly, laughingly through their teens, cutting the rest of us dead. A zest for life is remarkable for its absence. The hurt and disillusionment which the sensitive and intelligent young should experience when they begin to take a good look around, does not fire them with reforming zeal, heat them up so that they want to avenge the aggrieved. It heats them up, and they melt with self-pity. And the love on their love buttons is the kind of love that is so far from being intoxicating, so unlike the torment night and day of the beat, beat, beat of the tom-tom and the tick-tick-tock of the stately clock, that they turn away bored from that, to get their kicks from drugs.

The anonymous daughter above-mentioned who has the normal and natural taste of a teenager for exploring the subject of love and its manifold meanings, has likewise a normal and natural taste for testing the endurance of the mother.

"Suppose I were to say to you, Mother, I must have contraceptive advice. If you don't help me, nobody else will because I am too young. Suppose I said I were in love, and I didn't see why I shouldn't go all the way. And I told you that I would go ahead anyway, and it would be your fault if I had a baby if you wouldn't help me. (*pause*) Wouldn't it?"

Now right at this juncture my inclination to bawl, "Ah, come on!" is nearly irrepressible; and by the time Nora is in her teens and is setting me up like this, I'll probably only be capable of emitting a low hebetating sound like a lonely little motor boat at the other end of the lake. However, I am glad to report I acquitted myself. I began philosophically and ineffectually, and continued in this familiar self-depleting way and then—click—I had crossed over from patience to impatience, also familiar, and I said in a voice a bit steely: "Listen, X, dear. You want to know when a girl is old enough for this kind of intimate relationship? I'll tell you when. When she is mature enough to keep it to herself and to protect herself from any unwonted consequences. It is very far from being the sort of thing one shares with one's mother. We cannot say flatly that you must never have a love affair, but we do say flatly that there should be no accidents."

"But if I did have an accident?" she asked in a gentle, worried way, "and I came home to you and daddy, how would you feel?"

"We would be furious! We'd be so annoyed at your incompetence!" I said already annoyed.

"That is the answer," she announced majestically. "I accept that." And I felt I had been printed firmly with a stamp of approval—not a familiar feeling.

CHAPTER 14

Under the Rose

Speak in French when you can't think of the English for a thing—turn out your toes when you walk—and remember who you are!

Alice Through the Looking-Glass

At this very moment on my desk there is a single red rose past the height of its bloom in a Danish bud vase. (I have to raise my own eyebrow as I have to buy my own rose.) The underside of this rose, which I have been staring at for some time, is unremarkable. It looks like the underside of a rose and is disappointing if you are trying to find in the unfading velvet rose-red, in the curl of the petals, a clue to why things done, things told in secret, are called *sub rosa*. It is better to look in the dictionary. "The rose being anciently a symbol of secrecy (was) hung up at entertainments as a token that nothing there said was to be divulged."

The rose is anciently and modernly a symbol so widely borrowed for such diverse uses that Gertrude Stein felt the need to restore its identity. Rose is a rose is a rose.

151

Meanwhile, what is now described as going on under the rose is presumed to be tainted. Secret is a secret is a secret is no more the meaning of *sub rosa*. We take it that what happens *sub rosa* is not merely secret but immoral or illegal or shameful in some other way. I would like to restore to the meaning of *sub rosa* the innocence—if indeed it ever had an innocence—of that simple secrecy that justifies itself when *not* to tell is kinder and wiser than to tell. I am gunning for that ferocious pursuit of the truth, the telling all, the belief that man must be rid of all his illusions if he is ever to save himself. It is a pursuit that confuses, it seems to me, what is under the rock and what is under the rose.

What is under the rock is the fear and hate that breed in dark and airless places, dark and airless minds. It is the sort of unenlightenment that produces jingoism and the white backlash. Ignorance that is negative, in which only meager and primitive understanding grows, is the kind that lies under the rock. Lift the rock. Lift all those rocks.

But what lies under the rose may be something else. It is not black and airless under the rose. There is a subtle half-light, and hovering in that tinted shadow, the outlines not clearly defined, are all the intellectual and moral doubts and uncertainties, most of the meaning of life, not to put too fine a point on it. I would put contrariety and dilemma there. I would put grace, tact, good manners, discretion, all those minor virtues. Taste is surely there. The decision to keep something to yourself, *not* to tell, *not* to confess, is made there. It's where secrets are honored. Lifting the rose is different from lifting the rock.

Now I am using the device of the rose to rescue, in particular, the good name of Good Manners. Their value as minor virtues has depreciated sadly these last twenty years under the double charge that they are both hypocritical and undemocratic. I don't for a moment subscribe

152

to either aspect of the indictment, for I believe that the detection of hypocrisy in good manners is descried by the previously mentioned zeal in pursuit of truth, which pursuit I'm not going to pursue. Of course it is true that adolescents also turn upon good manners as hypocritical, as veneer designed to conceal the unloveliness of what we really are; but as they grow older they may be expected to hear the secret beauty in a soft answer, feel the implicit kindness offered in a pleasant appearance. For I believe that good manners are a social kindness, a part of caring for what is outside yourself, and that the exercise, the habit of caring, is good for the inside of yourself as well. Qua mother I pass them along with great assurance—this, in spite of noting how uncombed and disorderly and dirty and unladylike and ungentlemanly one's own dear children can't wait to become.

I comforted myself that they would hold what they had learned in abeyance and would reapply their knowledge when they emerged into adult life. We know the young need to break away, to establish their own identities, and the present generation had hit on this great and successful way to outrage us, as I saw it. Nothing more complicated. I admired their sureness in this respect, the true feeling they had for Provocation. In any case, I never thought of their looking grubby as being related to our looking grubby.

But consider this statement by Erik Erikson that I ran across in the *Times* one day: "The values of any new generation do not spring full blown from their heads; they are already there, inherent if not clearly articulated, in the older generation. . . . The much discussed generation gap is just another way of saying that the younger generation makes overt what the older generation represses."

Pondering upon the proposition that values do not

spring full blown, I have come to the conclusion that the depreciation of good manners is not a new social phenomenon promoted by beatniks, hippies, and the New Left, but derives from the indifference and unkindness that their elders have been cultivating for some time. On reflection I think it is possible that the horror that greeted the ladies' wearing slacks after World War II was prophetic horror after all—Pandora's pants. A casual, democratic age, a "Come as you are" age has spread in some unbeautiful directions. Is there an element of repressed hostility and contempt for our society in the very "casualness" with which we, who are older, appear in the community?

Travel through the country, visit any public place, and there you will find the American people of every age looking terrible. The mature eye has had to make innumerable hasty adjustments to what is evidently acceptable, and it has come to this, that group for group older people don't look any more appealing than the young. I believe the single difference is that the young have stopped washing—their *coup de grace*. It has certainly become unremarkable, upon stopping at a restaurant on a thruway, to find that the lady sitting at the next table has her hair rolled up in pink plastic curlers. Her indifference to the impression she makes on other people does not seem very repressed. Evidently her concern has shrunk to whoever it is she will meet at the end of the day. Everybody else, the people in her community, on her travels, the rest of America, in fact, seems to have been blotted out of consequence.

But I don't think this is altogether true. Personally she probably has some caring left in her, but national *esprit de corps* being so low she has missed the signals. I think if she looked up at the counter and saw two dirty, stringy-looking hippies just off the motorbike picking up french fried potatoes with their fingers (the way I do), she would be truly appalled and angry at the sight they made. I believe she would never dream of leaving the house *dirty*, in torn jeans and raveling sweater. But meanwhile the two hippies would no doubt return the compliment. A hippie girl would *never* appear in pink plastic—nor a hippie boy, I'd better say.

What is "inherent and not clearly articulated" in the dishabille of older people is a sulky rejection of society, and a cradling of the self, that become overt in the behavior of many of today's adolescents. But there are distinctions worth noting between our clean curlers and their dirty hair. Hippie manners and appearance may be an expression of contempt for the rest of society, but they are simultaneously an expression of fellowship for those who are like-minded. I doubt that two ladies sporting pink plastic curlers who notice each other in a public place, experience some little connecting trill of sisterhood. Curlers are not a sign of camaraderie, not a sign of Like reaching out for Like. They are a sign of the contrary.

When I was just a plain mother, and before I became an environmentalist, I anyway intuitively believed that my teaching good manners to my children was a necessary part of the structural apparatus for their growing upward. I don't see myself as hypocritical—superstitious or ridiculous, sometimes, but not hypocritical. Some of the structure I build with bamboo shoots and raffia. For instance, it rattled me that the girls would continue to hold their forks in their left hand here at home, whereas when they ate that way in Europe, where it is proper, it didn't. Finally I made them switch, and they said, but why? But how do I know why? How do I know, fortress of confidence that I am, which piece of trivia is going to pull me down? It's a kind of knocking wood, or, more aptly, knocking raffia. Meanwhile Nora is left-handed and eats with her left hand, and it doesn't bother me a bit. To be intimidated by this kind of manneristic proscription is pitiful, but then fork-switching isn't what I mean by good manners.

As an *environmentalist* I see each one of us, at the very least, as a part of the decor of life for others. Because it has become a jammed world, we are bound, I believe, to be as attractive, as *soothing* a part of the scene as is possible, and the test and function of good manners are whether they reduce human abrasion. I don't think it is a very small thing that whatever piece of earth you are traversing at the moment, you are not an offense to the eye, and are not leaving a trail of debris. I have found that a quite little child enjoys *not* littering. It is consistent with his belief that the world is his. And the other day I was amused to see how Nora accepted the efficacy of manners in the easing of her unnerved mother.

"When you come home from school," I told her one noon, "there's going to be somebody with me, and I want you to remember to say 'How do you do?'"

"Oh, no, I'm going to say 'Hello, Cuckoohead!'" and she laughed at her great joke.

"Listen, old girl," I said, firmish, something of my tension coming through. "It means a lot to me that you should say 'How do you do?' to this man, and I hope you will do it."

"Oh, well," she said casually, "if it means a lot, I'll say it."

And that afternoon she boomed through the door, placed herself foursquare before us, and announced clearly, 'How do you do?' three times, all grinning joy and mischief, treading the line with care to satisfy us both, mother and child.

Manners are based upon caring about what you look like from the outside, and to the extent that they work for you in a helpful way they offer forbearance, and they ask for forbearance in return. This I believe to be a Good Thing, and a lot better than that overprized virtue of frankness. To be frank, to strip away illusions, to tell somebody the whole truth as far as you are able, is only excusable in moments of honest fury, or when the other person (in *his* opinion) will really derive some benefit, which is rare. Cool frankness, however, nearly always springs out from self-admiration or self-pity, or some other aspect of the beloved you. I realize the contemporary world of arts and letters has been gung-ho for frankness for some time now, for open, painful confrontation with what is ugly, diseased, and depraved in the human condition, as if civilization was the greatest rock of all and what was crawling, white, and maggotty under it was the only reality, the only human reality. Put that rock back down! That's a rose! For me civilization is a rose. I suppose it is more evidence that I live in "the wrong time and the wrong place," as Ella sings, and as I have had more than one occasion to think.

All this artistic raw confrontation has been very instructive in some ways which I won't examine, but for mothers it hasn't been such a help. I wondered, while I watched George and Martha skin each other alive in the movie version of *Who's Afraid of Virginia Woolf?* should I trudge home thinking, Alas, that is a slice of life and there is a message in it that I must pass along? Actually, I had two other alases, one being Alas, this is not a slice of life but a biopsy of diseased tissue, and two, Alas, this is a very long movie. Perhaps it is only fair to identify myself artistically as one who finds movies very long these days.

In view of what I take to be the Art World's overlong absorption with depravity, I recommend that mothers, being of a naturally philistine disposition, ought to be jollied along in order to keep alive the old notions about how nice it is to watch your language, and pull your dress down, and keep your opinions to yourself sometimes. "Tact, Virginia? (or tact, little Martha?) Yes, there really is a usefulness and kindness and beauty to tact." It is true that now they have discovered lust, hot old lust, that the warming qualities in tact and humor—merely warming, not far-out hot—aren't really box office. But for the stage on which our children are likely to play out their lives, where they will have *real* babies and the more pedestrian pains and tensions, it's a *real* kindness to teach them good manners.

Now as to the imputation that good manners are undemocratic, I resist that with an older, deeper part of my being. The implication is that manners maketh the man who maketh it upward in the world. Perhaps it is due to my having grown up in the Bronx, where the belief in upward mobility escalated steadily through its landscape, that I look upon good manners as being extremely democratic, extremely. They were widely cultivated because they paid the passage for everybody on the way up, and everybody was. The Bronx was a true community with a shared goal: to get out and move to Manhattan. I must except my mother, however, who liked living in the Bronx, a very sophisticated pose this was—but she pulled it off.

Though I grew up in the Bronx I did not wander lovingly through it, did not sighing linger in it, and ever since I left I've thought of it as something that can be successfully bypassed on the way to Manhattan. Nonetheless, I owe to it a belief in progress through Acquiring the Graces, an election open to all. This was an American attitude our patriotic borough embraced a hundred per cent in a pre-complicated era, before psychological and racial inequity were uncovered. Her children were imbued with it, and when they left her behind, it was out of sight, out of mind. I am imbued with it still, and I send a little paean to her in gratitude.

Oh, when I think of the sure hand with good manners my mother had—how her authority rested upon the majesty of the whole royal house of Windsor! Queen Elizabeth and I grew up together. Although the Bronx was among the more remote of her father's enclaves my mother no less firmly charted the course of my privileges by the course of the privileges of the elder princess of England. First pair of silk stockings under the tree for her, first pair under the tree for me. Lipstick for her, lipstick for me. I always liked Elizabeth, shared her struggle.

We are both mothers of several children now, but we have lost touch. This is too bad because I have no yardstick by which to mete out permissions to my own young, and it would be handy to know what's going on over there in Buckingham Palace. What time does Charles have to be in at night? Did Anne really wear white socks and Mary Janes until she was 14? May she come down to supper with her hair rolled up in empty frozen orange juice cans?

Probably in the long run it is a good thing I don't belong to the upper classes. I would let our side down badly. I have a strong tendency toward what Darwin calls reversion. It is one of those things he says just happens to some individuals—they revert. Everybody else is improving on account of natural selection, but they revert. My manners, though in large part royal, are in large part irrelevant to the needs of my children, and what I am passing on to them is an earthier, less aristocratic mixture, and I hope it will prove to be more forthright in meeting the anguished needs of today's world.

The airs and graces I learned were sufficient to cope with life before World War II, but they are not sufficient to life before World War III. They must be supplemented by those minor virtues: tact, patience, discretion, circumspection (the synonyms are reinforcement), and humor, handiest of all, humor. These are the implements of interior grace. These are the gentilities you need, not only out in society, but more importantly inside yourself, to ease the strain of an era marked by contradictions. They weren't necessary in the Bronx of my childhood when there were no contradictions.

CHAPTER 15

Pornography and Pushing

Doctrinaires are the vultures of principle. They feed upon a principle after it is dead.

LLOYD GEORGE

No doubt I do live in the wrong time and the wrong place. Where I am a type that's really *in,* my chin thrust farthest out, my self a solid member of the avant-garde, is London in about 1900. Look how excited I get about Ibsen. I could have been a Shavian and a Fabian. So far from feeling contempt for Picasso's new Blue Period I would have been absolutely sent by it. In 1900 I would have been With It. They'd all have been speaking to me. J. S. Mill would have answered all my questions. Talk about bliss in that dawn to be alive, I wasn't even born.

My life has been an adjustment to this misplacement of me in history. I yearn to belong to my age, to wrap my arms around a faith, swear fealty to the purest Freedom, for instance: *know* that Mill has said the final word forever. If everybody believed in Jesus Christ, or if everybody believed in Historical Materialism, or Democracy, or Absolute Intellectual Freedom, if everybody would just look straight at the world through one pair of eyes, the evil forces would give up. Wouldn't they, though.

What I believe about absolute intellectual freedom is that it is a slogan and not a solution. It raises a lot of problems. Freedom is never simple, always invites abuse and license, and tends to be committed to our trust arm in arm with Responsibility. But it is in the special case of Freedom of the Press, Freedom from Censorship, that one hopes to find freedom from caveats. One wants to worship the graven image, deify the printed word. That is to say, when an issue arises in connection with the freedom of the press, such as the right of the pornographer to make an honest living, I would dearly love to stand unflinching and true to my banner: No Censorship. As it was, I wobbled. When the Supreme Court decided against the unlimited right to advertise and circulate this particular genre of printed matter, I found that I read the majority decision with sympathy. Having been, up to that moment, regarded as an equal in the ranks of that happy breed of unimpeachable liberals in the Elm Street area, I found myself suddenly alone, outside, looking around for another falterer and not finding anybody. Outside, chin in, I stood while they stripped me of my rank and who knows whether tears were in my eyes?

It may be difficult to believe, but the only thing I find irresistibly intriguing about pornography is this problem it poses for those who like to believe they have an open mind: and I like to believe it about myself. All of a sudden everybody began writing about pornography except mothers (until now) and it is possible, ignoble and diminishing as the subject is, that it is anyhow among those ideas whose time has come. As far as I understand it, there were two prime movers who brought pornography to its star position in the think magazines. The first was

General De Gaulle. In defense of the virtue of La Belle Marianne, that beautiful girl, President De Gaulle stopped the presses of her leading publisher of dirty books, one of the world's great sources, it seems, and the publisher, hurt, bewildered, and finding himself homeless, went where all the world's homeless want to go. He came to us. The other is the well known case of the American publisher who fought for freedom all the way to the Supreme Court and lost.

The question of boundless freedom only comes up at the boundary, and pornography is *the* guerrilla movement in that outlying area, and that's why this subject became topical for intellectuals. They suffered. As it makes an intellectual quite sick to defend censorship of any kind, and as it often makes him quite sick to read pornography for signs of literary value as well, he ends up somewhat groggy, espousing a sort of open-ended permissivism, as if to say, "Bless me if we aren't about to arrive at that glorious condition of Total Sexual Freedom shudder."

Meanwhile the publishers of pornography cried out against their persecutors with an ardor that brought little soblets to the throat. Their remarks on the spiritual, legal, cultural, and hygienic value of pornography were atremble with Liberty and Freedom, and were as pure, in the way of titillation, as a Lenten tract. It is amazing that on this at least in part ludicrous subject how short of humor one can be. Nothing about their extremely profitable profession interests them less than the money. Public Service is their field, the healthy, liberated personality their only care. They belong to the company of great martyrs, and when the court rocked the intellectual world by finding against the American publisher, in spite of this fine feeling, that world placed him firmly with the brotherhood of Ridley and Latimer: Latimer, who belonged to an era when they burned people *and* books, and who while being burned alive for heresy in 1555 cried out, "We shall this day light such a candle, by God's grace, in England, as I trust shall never be put out." It got hard to remember that the underlying issue was the pushing of obscene material.

I would like to believe, but do not believe, that the circulation of pornography among consenting adults harms no one and that it's only the Paul Prys and Sulky Sues who, out of spite and envy, make such a howl. In fact, the case against the harmlessness of this genre is very strong. Pornography, it seems, is not simply composed of dazzling descriptions of sexual activity, but of that activity intimately and crucially involved with sadism and with human debasement. It is the opinion of the English critic, George Steiner, that so much of erotica sounds eerily like the reports from the Nazi death camps as to make one question whether there is a causal relationship. "We do not live in abstract eternity," he reminds us. "We live in a period of history marked by an explosion of mass sadism and by the methodical reversion of many political communities to the use of torture."

There seems to be no question at all that the ghastly Moors murders were inspired by the reading of pornographic-sadistic books. Pamela Hansford Johnson, who was sent to the trial to cover this case, was so appalled by the evident cause and effect of reading Sade on the minds of the killers that she felt herself forced to reopen the question of absolute artistic freedom. Can the responsibility of an author-artist for, in this instance, the torture of children, by the manipulation of imagination and the sharpening of perverse appetites, any longer be dismissed as unconnected, or unproved, or irrelevant? Ought the consequences of such manipulation of unhinged persons —that is to say, those who are not "normal" or not "average," whoever they are, or whoever we are—remain entirely beyond the consideration of law in a free society?

I was very moved by reading the decision of Judge John M. Woolsey freeing *Ulysses* for publication in the United States and from the label of pornography. It was written in 1933 and reprinted as a foreword to the Modern Library edition, and its conclusion rests upon the belief that this difficult book would not unduly "stir the sex impulses" of the normal man. "Whether a particular book would tend to excite such (sex) impulses and thought must be tested by the Court's opinion as to its effect on a person with average sex instincts—what the French would call *l'homme moyen sensuel*—who plays, in this branch of legal inquiry, the same role of hypothetical reagent as does the 'reasonable man' in the law of torts and 'the man learned in the art' on questions of invention in patent law."

Judge Woolsey's decision, which is enlightened and sensitive, bears the hallmark of an earlier era. He cannot have imagined a Nazi Germany, or the molding of whole societies by the electronic wonders of the communications industry. Nor could he have himself experienced the formidable invasion into the privacy of the home of public relations techniques and advertising schemes—not only from radio and television, but solicitation by telephone and by direct mail.

It is hard to believe that a taste for sadism and debasement, generously satisfied, will not leave the humane and noble elements in a man's nature undernourished. Still, a man's nature is to some degree unalterable, something that can be said about each of us. We are what we are, and to the extent that we differ from the popular preference, why, we should be cherished, or understood, or simply left alone. Toleration of what we are, that is, should enjoy the widest latitude. Hope for what our children can become, for what heights human nature can achieve—that engages a different department of man's thinking.

Meanwhile to tolerate the differences in our nature is not the same as to tolerate the open and lucrative traffic in pornography that circles around ever more boldly, looking for "consenting adults." As with illicit drugs, the prod of financial profit is a powerful motive to create new customers for one's products. The drumming up of trade will be only as discrete as the law makes it be. One can see that in spite of the law the illegal drug business is flourishing. But at least there aren't "pot" ads in your friendly drug store. Not yet.

And here we arrive at the chain of associations which stays the hand and even the mind of a liberal when he is faced with the question of whether there is anything to do about pornography. For "drug store" brings to mind the dirty paperbacks you can get there, and thence to the civic groups determined to clean them up, shockingly certain that their own literary judgment is sufficient to the determination of what is good and what is bad, and before you know it you are fellow traveling with the vigilantes.

That the Supreme Court decided there was such a thing as obscene material "utterly without redeeming social value," appalled our academic community. "Frankly, I'm against censorship of any kind," was the single response, and I must say I found it quite uncharitable of people to regard the decision as a body blow to literature and intellectual freedom. Why did they count it nothing that the Commonwealth of Massachusetts, home of book-banning as well as our home too, was quite firmly rapped for proscribing *Fanny Hill* as obscene? *Fanny Hill* is *not* "utterly without redeeming social value." It doesn't matter, the court contended, how much social value (or literary merit or sociological significance or whatever) a book has. It can only be declared obscene if it is utterly without it: utterly—a thorough, purging, satisfactory word. The door is still open for Lady Chatterley and her gamekeeper and Henry Miller and his younger self to walk in easily. What the court allowed was that society's desire to protect its moral standards (however questionable those standards may be) from blatant mockery and assault by *panderers* was not utterly irrelevant.

The association of liberty with anarchy and irresponsibility remains on the frontier of liberal thought, and very few intellectuals like to go out to the edges of their own territory to see what the actual problems are. I know it is the female in me that responds in alarm. I superintend the development of the new generation, or five members of it, and confronted by the determined abolition of social standards, the discarding of traditional social amenities, I see not a new freedom but a new tyranny rising.

On the subject of *le porno*, as the French call it, I am not too well read—not because I am immune—certainly I am aware they have a little something for housewives, but, you know, that sort of stuff is liable to cut one's taste for cooking and cleaning. I do notice that the defense of pornography is invariably coupled with a glib acceptance of homosexuality. The gay way this goes is that homosexuality is just one more variation on human relationships, something the Greeks knew was perfectly natural but that Christianity arbitrarily proscribed as unsuitable for the proliferation of Christians—but which now that we are in an era of dangerous overpopulation is a relationship that does more to benefit the Human Cause than most. There is no recognition here that to be a homosexual is to be unfortunate or unhappy or unhealthy. Judgment is next door to persecution.

Instinctively, or perhaps irrationally, I react against this facile permissivism. It is my daily round forever to wrestle with the difficulty of teaching my children simultaneously to acquire high personal standards and meanwhile to keep an open mind. But that is not a difficulty confined to mothers. I cannot believe that it is blind prejudice that prevents me from presenting homosexuality as one of life's alternatives, as, in the case of careers, one would present law or medicine. My stake is in family life, and when I read about homosexuals that "they do not participate in the saga which is the normal life of man. Instead they live all their lives arrested, as it were, in the same situation . . .," I am swept by the pity of it. I saw once the results of a discrete poll taken in a large homosexual community. Among those asked whether, if it were possible, they would wish to change, 97 per cent said they would not. This seemed to reflect considerable composure and satisfaction, and indicated that my pity was irrelevant. Until the last question. When asked if he had a son would he want him to be a homosexual too, 2 per cent said yes. I don't believe it is only harassment by society that accounts for this response. Harassment is nasty. But a hearty welcome is crazy. Here again opinion is polarized, whereas the closest one can come to justice and kindness will be an inexplicit, subtle, wavering line, off-center, toward the left.

It is handsome to stand up for freedom for pornography and equality for perversion, and think no more about it. It swells the heart if it doesn't satisfy the mind, again because we do not live in "abstract eternity." I live now in an era of swift social change and must anyhow teach my children ageless moral values and ethical principles, and I am no island. I cannot stand alone here. We are a family, part of a community within a small city inside a vast country, and I need the whole of it to stand more or less firmly behind my (nobler) self. And the law, while on the one side it must protect the individual rights of the least consequential and attractive among us, must, on the other, sufficiently support the body of our diverse traditional attitudes and beliefs, those that are worthy, so that we are not badly demoralized by the knocking down of all our guideposts. It is good to knock down segregation, dismantle its legal support and encouragement of injustice, for instance, but I believe it would have been wrong to let loose all restraints upon pornography because it would have been a crucially demoralizing act. If large minds do not address themselves to the progressive fragmentation of our lives, there'll soon be a field day for the small minds.

But large minds have. The Supreme Court, by placing restraints upon "the commercial exploitation of erotica solely for the sake of their prurient appeal" has touched the very problems that reach down into my family and my community. We do not care what consenting adults do or what they read in privacy and with discretion. We are dismayed by the increasing confidence of the *panderers,* and by the increasing boldness of their pandering to what the court calls our "widespread weakness for titillation by pornography." For the panderers are as interested in their sales volume as any growth industry, and there is hardly one among us who cannot be considered a potential customer. We are all accustomed to the idea that a sexual motif will decorate the cover of every magazine through model cars and needlework, through the "vast wasteland" that is television, that it will beckon you to every movie, particularly Biblical (to compensate). What the court calls "the leer of the sensualist" (originally Judge Woolsey's phrase) is what sells the gross national product.

The leer of the sensualist is extremely provocative and the children of the community see it all over the place; and it softens them up, as it softens us all, in respect to the ancient rules of self-discipline. Julie and Maggie, out of the neighborhood school, tootle off in the mornings to a world in which forbidden fruits are rotting on the vine. I used to worry about high-school life with its smoking and drinking and cars to whisk the half-grown out of supervision. Now it is worse; it is drugs. All the old fruits were too easy to reach, too abundant, spoiled.

It is difficult for our communities to protect themselves when the allure of their moral standards is to be matched against that leer. And besides, the word "community" itself disguises the fact that we are disconnected from one another, separate households, hesitant parents, nervous teachers, the Law, all little whirls of worry about where we stand in respect to the rights of others. We have outgrown the tribal chief, the Biblical judge; we are so many scattered elders wandering in the wilderness.

I have said that my stake is in family life, and that everybody's stake is, and that technology cannot supplant the family. But it can affect the future of an unwanted or neglected child. Where the nurturing of a child's spirit is seriously deficient, it does not let that child die from undernourishment. It allows him to live on, to become delinquent or destructive, or lonely and wretched, sick to the end of his long, long life. It contributes to the great and growing numbers of people with grossly damaged sensibilities, partial human beings with maimed minds simply incapable of even dreaming dreams of glory, of achievement, of hope and joy, the binding human dreams.

The nightmare future societies of deadened, amoral, robotlike manipulable people that Aldous Huxley and George Orwell describe derive from the evil offices of government, of thought control and the monolithic state, of the eradication of freedom. But future societies may become benighted abruptly and haplessly by the acquisition of total freedom from the Sense of Community—that sense of community that has historically supported our inner strength by outer leverage. In a community or a nation, a giving up, a passive indifference, the loss of all rapport must sap the family, break the offspring.

The family is guide to the infant, to the schoolboy with his satchel, with luck through the first two decades of life, standing particularly firm for wisdom, conscience, and high values during adolescence so that a boy will not yield to a weak choice and fritter away the promise in his life. As an army marches on its stomach, so a nation's future rests on the sturdiness of family life.

And so the court in this decision, it seems to me, has at once considered the right of the living generations to their freedom, and the right of future generations to a sufficient promise of health so that they in their turn may enjoy freedom too. The court, especially now when old religions and old ways have lost their command over us, represents our national wisdom. This wisdom is composite and a wellspring, and is fed not only by the brilliance of Locke, Jefferson, and Mill but from older Judeo-Christian sources and from new insights, from Freud and a fresh awareness of how delicate and complex are the mind and spirit of man, how subtle are the processes of human growth.

What to one person is compassionate concern is to another unwarranted interference. But some lines have been drawn before this. We have long recognized that America is not just so many segments of private property side by side, where a man may be as wanton as he wishes with what's his own, so long as he does not start ravaging what's somebody else's. Conservation is not a brand new thought, born of our panic over poisoning our water supply or running out of arable land. We see that the living have this earth in trust, that none of us is morally free to despoil it. On this principle, out of regard to our posterity, we set restraints, because we know how it goes without standards.

So for the land, so for the people.

The earth for its own sake, man for his own sake.

And if it matter what manner of man we will be, it matters how we nurture our young, how gracious, how hospitable their environment is.

CHAPTER 16

The Intellectual Community and the Young

All that is human must retrograde if it do not advance.
EDWARD GIBBON

Utterly. You can be utterly without it; but perhaps not utterly with it. Things can be utterly false, but can things be utterly true? In the affirmative it is a word that is likely to be used as hyperbole unless you have some reason to say water is utterly wet. In regard to printed matter, something utterly without redeeming value is going to be hard to find, and the Court's decision has no doubt caused the publisher of pornography to think of adding a value-redeeming editor to his staff.

Meanwhile this particular decision gratified no one, if you don't count me. The intellectual community was aggrieved at the one end of the stick, and America's mothers, at the other, could hardly draw comfort from a protective fence that looked all gate. Now this stick is my stick, because I live in an intellectual community, and my hope and respect rest with the fineness of mind that is nurtured in it, that will see us lost in the wilderness and lead us out. As a woman I believe that our environment, the safety of our nesting places, are imperiled. The apple has been bitten again. Once more it is more than we can chew.

Among the swift changes of this age that is pleasant is the fact that one can speak at all of an intellectual community in this country. In the early fifties, during the first McCarthy period, it seemed hardly to exist beyond little ineffectual fragments and isolated conclaves, and it certainly led no counterforce against its enemy. I remember people talking ruefully of the forceful intellectual communities of other countries, of France and England, for examples, and attributing their strength to the smallness of the country and the centrality of university life. There was the London-Oxbridge axis, and there was the Sorbonne right in Paris. But the Communications Revolution and the jet plane have canceled the distances and given America a head, and that is certainly encouraging when you look back on the headlessness of before.

But to look this head square in the eye is to see that the media that have made it possible have also in part molded it. The intellectual community is subject to the same forces that polarize everything today. It is made to appear a kind of monolithic left wing block. It is certainly on the left, but then nearly all thought, all paths of creative thinking, tend to open into the future, to expand toward compassion and the assumption of responsibility, away from laissez-faire and toward positive efforts to relieve man's suffering. One may associate a kindly liberalism with the word "left" but at its narrowest the left becomes fascistic. It is a concept that contains this contradiction.

It is a huge concept now that has even taken over the middle of the road; so much so that you are either in it or you're a fanatic, and what you have over there on the right is not a philosophy but an emotional problem. What the media do is to present this intellectual community, this commodious left, to the world at large as a single-minded, if not simple-minded, unit. They bring unity to intellectual disparity, they reduce it, simplify it, and in the end, eliminate this disparity because it is the only way they can handle it. It is the only way the communications industry seems able to communicate.

The distortion is so ramified and so witless it is impossible to cope with it. And members of the intellectual community themselves are influenced by this simplified image and find themselves pushed into absolute positions, helpless before the force of polarization. It is too mindless to be for war today, so one is for peace. One is for racial and sexual equality, against censorship. All the thinking, the exploration, the attacks and defenses that concern these issues inside the intellectual community—and there are fierce divisions—are not directed against the logic of those who believe in dropping napalm, or in the inherent inferiority of blacks and women, or in censorship. No logic is over there, no respect is wasted on that side. It is within the expansive bracket of the left that all the fierce divisions exist.

For the outside it has all been boiled down to a sort of doctrinaire liberalism edited by the doctrinaire liberals and a hard core of hard social scientists, true believers who do indeed exist and whose messages appear uncomplicated and eye-catching, and therefore tailored for communication. These spokesmen see the nonintellectual world reacting with a kind of homogenized bigotry against enlightenment and against a broadening of attitudes on every critical issue that presses down upon us. These are the little gods who would send the flood and drown it all, and let man start fresh, cleansed of his old repressive taboos, his hounding myths.

There is an elitist strain to the purer intellectual liberal. In the name of individual integrity, freedom, and equality he seems ready to have each man sink or swim, regardless of his muscles and his wind, but this doctrine does not take proper account of human interaction with environment. As the traditional moral and ethical landmarks of our lives are being washed away, the salient fact of our environment becomes the rising flood, and when we feel the waters at our armpits, why, we flounder. We should rejoice in the liberation of our uniqueness and the opportunities for honest development, but we don't. We flounder.

I resist where I can the force of polarization, but there are times when one must stand up and be counted, and there I am, standing up for something I don't believe. If I had lived in Cambridge or San Francisco when the referendums were presented on Vietnam—should we immediately pull out of Vietnam?—I would have voted yes, but I could hardly have believed in such a simple resolution. I found myself forced to support the circulation of an otherwise indefensible sheet—utterly without redeeming value, I thought—that was being published locally, because the attack against it seemed mounted by harpies. They frightened me. There was no middle ground. Were I asked whether I believed the falling of the double standard to be a good thing or a bad thing, I would check good. And if I had to say, True or False, black violence in the ghetto seems to be necessary to affect social change—I would say False. Or would I say True? And none of these answers is accurate. They would not express the Sense of myself. All of them would be misleading. And if I refused to answer, looking after my own purity and integrity, why I fear the totals would be the sadder for it. If we are not drowned, or until we are drowned, we are swept in a current toward one bank or the other.

Do I want to welcome the emergence of an intellectual community only to discredit it? Oh, do I not. I honor its disunity, the disparities, the contradictions and variations that are its realest marks. As they are the realest marks of the household. I wish they were finished with bewailing the chaos, is all. There may have been no covenant with God, and that has been a disappointment, but the rainbow is still a sign of the order, beauty, and logic that have produced human consciousness. One might see in the rainbow a covenant with the rational mind. I admire that consciousness, the rational mind at its most developed and sensitive, and the people in whom it resides. Will those people rest content to glory in an evolutionary process that culminates in such a grand achievement as themselves, and drop the rest of us? I wish, instead, they would fan out through all that diversity, those contradictions, searching for the benignant forces in the environment that contributed to their own astonishing development in order to spread their species of humankind, let it triumph in the human struggle. It's the only democratic thing to do.

The real danger of the simple elitism that tends, falsely, I believe, to characterize the intellectual community is the very undemocratic nature of it. Intramurally those belonging are democratic right enough. They suffer each other gladly, sometimes with savage joy. But they look at the rest of society across a gulf, and they make the gulf wider. Inch by inch they have moved toward what I fear is an active policy of alienation, the cutting off of the new head. I fear it on principle, but there is a more intimate threat which I feel in common with all parents. We are

177

bringing up children in order to deliver them over into an academic milieu which is essentially separatist in its sympathies, and which more or less supports the schismatic bias in the younger generation. It supports it without making any appreciable effort to harness the goodwill and intelligence that is distributed (of course in less remarkable density) throughout the rest of the population so that we can understand better, cope better, live better.

Northampton is an academic community and for me it has been the most benign of environments, and Smith surely the wisest of colleges. There is inevitably some division between town and gown but the strain of separatism that I sense here is not local, but part of the national phenomenon. I've thought about it now and then while standing on line at the peace vigil that has been held at noon on Sundays throughout the Vietnam war. Tactically speaking, one ought to go down there, the men shaved, and in blue business suits (or is it gray now?), the ladies dressed for tea, the students looking like models for a poster that says Uncle Sam Needs You. Because the point isn't to persuade somebody like me. I am already on that side. I already believe that we could, if we would, if we *willed* it, pursue our self interest in foreign affairs on a higher, more sophisticated moral plane, commensurate with the higher, more sophisticated destruction we are able to wreak.

That Peace Vigil is a travesty of the proposition that the medium is the message. There we are lined up, glorying in our individual selves as reflected in our truly personalized costume, contemptuous of those who confuse a superficial appearance (our small thing) with a sound, deep understanding (our big thing), and we drive away all the customers.

We stand on a line but we won't draw a line, about dress, for instance. There are no rules and there is no leader. I am reminded of those Republicans who chose gladly to lose the election with Goldwater rather than to win with another candidate. What is a man profited if he shall gain the whole world and lose his own soul? It's an interesting question in a democratic society.

I very occasionally join that line, assuming a solemn and responsible pose, looking straight ahead of me across the wide Main Street and vaguely at the Boot Shop window, and I think, I wish Peg O'Brien were here and we could while away this long hour talking. But we do have one rule on this line. It is silence. It's really the only kind of rule we feel capable of making, a pure rule. You can be utterly silent. It may interfere with the right of the individual to chatter while vigiling, but it does not entail the difficulty that making a rule about dress, physical appearance, invites. Try to make a rule about clothes or tonsure and there you are, trying to draw a line.

Old as most of us are, it is youth that sets the tone of the vigil. Next to me, holding hands, are a flower person (f.) and a creep (m.) (a word I borrow from the vocabulary of my youth) and who is going to notice how safe and dowdy is my get-up as I pose sedately by their side. I draw in a deep breath of aggravation but it comes out tenderness. The fabric of our society may be suffering from rot but, out at the fringe, the two long-haired strands on the left remind me, they're looking for love and peace, a beautiful brace of values, a Christian brace. Too bad their love and peace rest on not caring.

Still under a tender spell, my mind picked up Not Caring and Permissive Child-Rearing, Alienation and Anything Goes like dropped stitches, and it knitted this parallel: in the bringing up of children permissivism sponsored an intimacy, a togetherness as it is called in mockery, that ought, if nothing else, to have left the young steeped in human warmth, permanently fastened by love to other members of mankind, but somehow it didn't. Somehow those young are at least as alienated as everybody else claims to be, and being articulate—or perhaps because they are articulate, they sound even more alienated. Now they are grown up, and as students— 40 per cent of the age group enters some form of what is roughly called higher education—they thereby effect a liaison with the intellectual community.

One understands, again no doubt through the distortion of the media, that undergraduate life on the campuses of the multiversities, for instance, is irrelevant to the needs of the individual and reinforces loneliness. Due to their vast numbers students are processed by an enormous administrative apparatus, and they feel processed. They don't find themselves in that sweet, deep loneliness that surprises your walk back from the library in the dusk over worn paths, that twines your being like ivy to the very stones of the buildings you pass. It is given to them instead to use the opportunity to feel communion while waiting for the elevator in the highrise dorm.

They feel alienated, detached from purpose and meaning, and their condition elicits enormous distress and concern from the intellectual community. More than that, it evokes from some members of the community a positive action, a rallying to them, a joining and embracing that should flood them with a sense of being cared for, that should warm them—but it doesn't. American society is corrupt and degenerate, cry the young. Isn't it ever, cry their sympathetic superiors. And the bond they create together is a bond of self-pity, of individual self-pity. And the fellowship in dissent which should bind them is broken by the unselectivity of dissent, as dissent sinks into a generalized contempt; and the comforting embrace of the elders aborts and becomes, by terrible mischance, a pandering to this ubiquitous self-pity, to everybody's lonely isolating self-pity.

Now the parallel I see in the permissive parent's embrace of the child and the permissive professor's embrace of the student, with the desired warmth and communal feeling *not* being transmitted, is that the justification for these two kinds of relationship rests upon the fiction that the partners in each instance are equal. The implication is that by this mandate of equalization you allow people to become closer to one another. But this fiction tampers with the meaning and function of time, with the time that accounts for the arc or continuum of human life from birth to death, and if I subscribe to this fiction that I, a mother, am equal to my child, I forfeit the sense of having evolved, having absorbed, gained, grown, of my being worth the trouble of having been born, and I deprive my child of that forward thrust of the soul toward his destiny.

And in like manner, to the extent that those who teach in the universities yield to the demoralizing forces and align themselves with the undiscriminating protest natural to the young—to the extent, that is, that they do not distinguish between strength and weakness, health and illness, a good law and a bad law—to that extent do they diminish themselves, too, shrink back to a simpler, less complicated plateau of growth where they can once more rejoice in oneness, in purity—the Law is an ass, Anything Goes, No Censorship—and what is the consequence to the student is that the pillars are brought down, the values and achievements of the human mind, those enormous structures, are leveled, the history of civilization is sunk behind them, there is no bridge to the future—there is no future. Time is lopped off fore and aft. The present is the only reality. To make bearable a present that is perpetual, you are probably well advised to drug yourself, chemically or sexually or however you can. Meanwhile if one considers love and caring, how they operate, it will be seen that they must move along a strand of time, that their dependency on time is among their chief characteristics.

It is a kind of strange dead end that we come to in our

American youth fixation. I have a picture in my mind of a whole generation of theory-reared babies growing larger and larger and as they attain great size on account of vitamins, and draw closer to their twenty-first birthdays, they begin to dig in their heels ever more fixedly, and when they arrive at their majority they refuse to move on, to leave childhood, to grow up.

Whatever was the intention and whatever have been the failures of my generation of parents I can testify with a whole heart that by the time that tiny precious thing becomes a college freshman you are more than ready to have him grow up. And where the intellectual community may fail you is when it is not tough, not tough-minded. It should look down upon a student body (so exceptionally nurtured) with great expectations that it will rise high; it should not buckle under the weight of adolescent protests, grievances, bullying, nor be humbly apologetic about being the establishment, nor, in the extreme cases referred to above, skit across the great divide of time, and join in youth's lament.

I don't support the status quo. I support the amendment of it by due process, and if I were to prescribe a major exercise for the American educational curriculum, it would be to retrace the arguments that command a man's allegiance to a government of laws, and not of men, and thereby send us all, through the years of our growing up, over the path that the progress of civilization has taken, where the word civilization means "advancement in social culture." I would start this program in kindergarten. The intent would not be to lower dissent or disobedience in the eyes of the people, but to raise them. Protest now, by the indiscriminate nature of its choice of grievances, is too often whiney and small. If you are going to disobey the law for moral reasons they should be large moral reasons, and you should have the stature to take the consequences. To ask permission to rebel is craven.

The structure of all of American society, not only of the academic community, should be cemented by great expectations. So with the structure of the household—great expectations are what one has for one's children. The world, the nation, the city, the block, the family, the self—the larger environments are linked to the smaller, it is our chain of life. The intellectual community fails us when it ignores this fact, with all the taunting contradictions that the fact hauls after it. I believe that if we had the will our society could maintain an apparatus of great empirical, amendable, temporal expectations, of social and legal expectations. Our individual energies would not then go toward reconciling the contradictions, or crying because we can't, but in reconciling ourselves to living with them, to living with chaos and order, while championing the latter. This throws each one of us back upon ourselves, to discriminate between large and small, to determine when one must stand up and be counted, and when, counting the cost in human pain, it is better to slip under the rose. For the large things you may go to jail or give your life. The small are weight on your conscience.

It occurs to me that the answer our teen-age daughter found satisfactory when, in regard to contraception she was asking (hypothetically) for permission to rebel, is the kind of hedging answer that will have to serve many kinds of deviation from the social norm. If one is going to be unfaithful, or have a homosexual experience, or smoke marijuana, or read pornography, isn't it maturing, toughening, to take the responsibility on oneself, rather than elevate each desire to a constitutional right? People shouldn't be hounded for their variations, but society, looking to the health and sanity of new generations, doesn't have to sponsor all variations indiscriminately.

Certainly there must lie some line between hounding and sponsorship.

A woman must feel her way through all this contrariety. That is the compendium of modern culture, and that is what she must transmit to her children. And the reason I have made an issue of this polarization of ideas and opinions is that it has a seriously depressing effect on a woman who is respectful of intellectual matters, who looks to the printed word for guidance in rearing herself or rearing her children. When too few alternatives are offered, she may be shunted off into a despair that is not her true destination.